D1539432

SPECTRUM®

Test Prep

Grade 4

Published by Spectrum®
An imprint of Carson-Dellosa Publishing LLC
Greensboro, North Carolina

Spectrum®
An imprint of Carson-Dellosa Publishing LLC
P.O. Box 35665
Greensboro, NC 27425 USA

ISBN 978-1-4838-1377-6

01-349147811

Table of Contents

What's Inside? 4

Test-Taking Strategies 5

Strategies for English Language Arts Tests . . 6

Reading: Literature

Explain and Support Inferences 7

Determine Theme and Summarize Text 9

Determine the Meaning of Words and Phrases in a Text 11

Describe Characters, Settings, and Events 13

Explain Differences Between Poetry, Drama, and Prose 15

Compare and Contrast Different Points of View . 19

Compare and Contrast Stories 22

Reading: Informational Text

Explain and Support Inferences 26

Determine the Theme and Summarize Text 28

Explain Historical, Scientific, and Technical Text . 31

Describe the Overall Structure of a Text 33

Compare Two Texts 35

Language

Determine the Meaning of Words and Phrases . . 39

Demonstrate Understanding of Figurative Language, Word Relationships, and Nuances 41

Writing

Write an Opinion Piece 43

Write an Informative/Explanatory Text 45

Write a Narrative 49

Understand Editing and Revising 51

Language Arts Strategy Review 53

Strategies for Mathematics Tests 57

Operations and Algebraic Thinking

Interpret a Multiplication Equation as a Comparison 58

Solve Multiplicative Comparison Problems: Multiply and Divide 59

Solve Multi-Step Problems: Add, Subtract, Multiply, and Divide 61

Find Factors and Multiples 63

Analyze Patterns 64

Numbers and Operations in Base Ten

Recognize Multi-Digit Whole Numbers 65

Multi-Digit Whole Numbers: Base-Ten Numerals, Number Names, Expanded Form 66

Round Numbers to 1,000,000 67

Add and Subtract Multi-Digit Whole Numbers . . 68

Multiply Whole Numbers Using Strategies 69

Numbers and Operations—Fractions

Find Equivalent Fractions 73

Compare Fractions 75

Compose and Decompose Fractions 77

Add and Subtract Mixed Numbers 79

Multiply a Fraction by a Whole Number 81

Change Fractions with Denominators of 10 to Equivalent Fractions with Denominators of 100 . 83

Use Decimal Notation for Fractions 84

Compare Decimals 85

Measurement

Understand Measurement Units 86

Solve Problems: Distance, Time, Volume, Mass, and Money 88

Measurement and Data

Solve Problems: Area 90

Solve Problems: Perimeter 91

Make a Line Plot and Solve Problems 92

Understand Angle Concepts and Measurement . 93

Geometry

Measuring Angles 94

Solve Problems: Unknown Angle Measures . . . 95

Identify Lines and Angles 97

Classify Two-Dimensional Figures 99

Identify Symmetry 101

Math Strategy Review 102

Answer Key 106

What's Inside?

Spectrum® Test Prep is designed to help you and your fourth grader prepare and plan for success on standardized tests.

Strategies

This workbook is structured around strategies. A strategy is a careful plan or method for achieving a particular goal, such as succeeding on a test. Strategies can be broad, providing ways to approach a test as a whole or a category of skills. Strategies can also be specific, providing step-by-step instructions on how to tackle a problem or offering guidelines on how to answer a question about a story. This workbook offers a set of broader strategies and very specific strategies. General test-taking strategies apply to all tests, and should be used to help prepare for the test. Specific strategies for English Language Arts and Mathematics tests are divided into larger categories of skills students will encounter, such as reading literature or performing calculations. On each practice page, you will find even more specific strategies that apply to the skills.

Test Tips

Test Tips are included throughout the practice page. While strategies offer a plan for answering test items, Test Tips offer ideas for how to apply each strategy or how to approach a type of question. There are Test Tips that apply to all tests and Test Tips for English Language Arts and Mathematics tests.

Practice Pages

The workbook is divided into two sections, English Language Arts and Mathematics. Each section has practice activities that have questions similar to those that will appear on standardized tests. Students should use a pencil to complete these activities.

Strategy Review Pages

Strategy review pages give your student an opportunity to review and practice important strategies in each content area. These strategies cover the important skills students will encounter on tests in English Language Arts and Mathematics.

Answer Key

Answers for all of the practice pages and strategy review pages are found in an answer key at the end of the book.

Test-Taking Strategies

Being prepared is key to doing your best on test day. Read the tips below to help you prepare for tests.

In the days before the test...

- Keep up on your reading, worksheets, and assignments. Completing all assigned work will help you be better prepared for the test.

- Don't wait until right before the test to review materials. Create a study schedule for the best result. That way, you can study a bit at a time and not all at once.

- Take advantage of sample items and practice tests. Complete these to practice for your test. If you run into concepts or skills that are new, ask a teacher or other adult.

The night before the test...

- Don't try to study everything all over again. If you've been studying in the days before the test, all you need the night before is a light review of your notes. Remind yourself of the key ideas and practice a few skills, but don't study late into the night.

- Make sure you have all the materials you will need for the test, such as pencils, paper, and a calculator. Check with your teacher to make sure you know what tools to bring. Having everything ready the night before will make the morning less stressful.

- Get a good night's sleep the night before the test. If you are well rested, you will be more alert and able to do your best.

On the day of the test...

- Don't skip breakfast. If you are hungry, you won't be thinking about the test. You'll be thinking about lunch.

- Make sure you have at least two sharpened pencils with you and any other tools needed.

- Read all directions carefully. Make sure you understand how you are supposed to answer each question.

- For multiple choice questions, read all the possible answers before choosing one. If you know that some answers are wrong, cross them off. Even if you have to guess, this will eliminate some wrong answers.

- Once you choose or write an answer, double check it by reading the question again. Confirm that your answer is correct.

- Answer every part of a question. If a question asks you to show your work or to explain how you arrived at an answer, make sure you include that information.

- If you are stuck on a question, or are unsure, mark it lightly with a pencil and move on. If you have time, you can come back. This is especially true on a timed test.

- Breathe! Remind yourself that you've prepared for the test and that you will do your best!

Strategies for English Language Arts Tests

Read the strategies below to learn more about how they work.

Use details from the text to make inferences, understand theme, and draw out meaning.
Writers carefully choose details to include in their writing. Every detail matters. Each one is included for a purpose. As you read stories, look for details that help you understand what the writer is saying about characters, events, and the overall meaning, or theme. As you read passages, look for details that give reasons that support any opinions or facts the writer shares, as well as the central or main idea.

Identify literary or structural elements and use them to understand the meaning of a text.
Writers use literary elements such as figurative language to bring more meaning to their writing. They choose a structure that reflects their purpose for writing. Read carefully for ways that these elements help you understand the meaning of a story, poem, or passage.

Look carefully at visuals such as illustrations, diagrams, or graphs to see how they connect to the text.
Visuals are always related to the text. It is up to readers to figure out the connection. Does the visual explain something that is difficult to say in words? Does it add detail? As you read stories and passages, look carefully at visuals to see what information they provide.

Reread texts to make comparisons, draw conclusions, or support inferences.
Every reader has his or her own ideas about a text. If you are asked to draw a conclusion about what the writer means or thinks, however, you need to rely on details in the text, not your own opinions. When you have drawn a conclusion or made an inference, reread the text to make sure you can support it with facts, examples, and other information from the text.

Use word clues in a text to identify its structure, to see how ideas in a text are related, and to clarify word meanings.
Some words are signals that a text has a particular structure. For example, the words *cause* and *because* often signal a cause-and-effect structure. You may also be able to use words as clues to the meaning of unfamiliar words.

When writing, use details to support, explain, or clarify your main ideas.
In persuasive and informational writing, it is important to make sure you support and explain each main idea with details. Facts, examples, and logical reasoning can all be used to make your main ideas strong and clear.

Use an outline to plan your writing.
Prewriting activities such as outlining can make writing clear and make your ideas easy to understand. A simple outline that lists main ideas or claims followed by their supporting details is enough to make your writing flow more easily.

Use transitions to show how ideas are related.
As you write, use transitions to help your reader follow your train of thought. You may know how your ideas are related, but readers need a little extra help! For example, the transition *As a result* shows that you are explaining a cause and an effect. The transitions *Next* and *Finally* help readers see that you are explaining a process or events that happen in a certain order.

Revise to make sure your writing is clear and makes sense. Then, edit to fix errors.
After you finish your draft, you may have time to revise and edit. First, revise to make sure your words say what you wanted them to say. Then, check spelling, capitalization, punctuation, and grammar to catch and fix errors.

English Language Arts

Explain and Support Inferences
Reading: Literature

DIRECTIONS: Read the story. Then, answer the questions.

WATERLAND

"Hurray!" cried Meghan. "Today is the day we're going to Waterland!" It was a hot July day, and Meghan's mom was taking her to cool off on the water slides. Meghan's new friend, Jake, was going too. Just then, Meghan's mom came out of her bedroom. She did not look very happy. "What's the matter, Mom? Are you afraid to get wet?" Meghan teased. "I'll bet you'll melt, just like the Wicked Witch of the West!"

Mrs. Millett didn't laugh at the joke. Instead, she told the kids that she wasn't feeling well. She was too tired to drive to the water park. Meghan and Jake were disappointed. "My mom has chronic fatigue syndrome," Meghan explained. "Her illness makes her really tired. She's still a great mom."

"Thank you, dear," said Mrs. Millett. "I'm too tired to drive, but I have an idea. You can make your own Waterland, and I'll rest in the lawn chair." Meghan and Jake set up three sprinklers. They dragged the play slide to the wading pool and aimed the sprinklers on the slide. Meghan and Jake got soaking wet. Mrs. Millett sat in a lawn chair and rested. The kids played all day.

"Thank you for being so understanding," Meghan's mom said. "Now, I feel better, but I'm really hot! There's only one cure for that." She stood under the sprinkler with all her clothes on. She was drenched from head to toe. Meghan laughed and said, "Now you have chronic wet syndrome." Mrs. Millett rewarded her daughter with a big, wet hug. It turned out to be a wonderful day after all at the backyard Waterland.

Strategy
As you read, pay attention to details from the story. Use the details to explain the story and to make inferences.

Test Tip
Use what you already know and the details from the story to make inferences.

1. How do you think Mrs. Millett feels about not being able to take the children to Waterland?

(A) She is glad she won't have to spend her whole day with children.

(B) She feels sorry for herself and is glad she got out of it.

(C) She is disappointed she can't take the children.

(D) She is hurt and confused.

2. In this story, *fatigue* means the same as _____.

(A) to be excited

(B) to be tired

(C) to be sad

(D) to be sick

Write how you know.

_____

_____

3. How do you think Meghan feels about her mother's illness?

_____

_____

_____

English Language Arts

Explain and Support Inferences
Reading: Literature

DIRECTIONS: Read the story. Then, answer the questions.

THE FIRST DAY

"I don't know about this, Mom." Henry frowned. It was the first day of school, and he was walking with his mom. "Maybe I should just stay home with you and start kindergarten next year." Henry's mom laughed and fluffed his hair with her hand. They continued up the path to school.

The path was curved with lots of trees on either side. The sun came down between the branches and lit Henry's mom's face. "You're going to love school! You get to learn fun new things and make a bunch of friends," she told him.

"Sadie's older brother said the teacher was mean and the math is hard, though!" Henry was ignoring his mom's comforting words.

They continued to walk up the path until they reached a bright red door, which led to a light blue hallway. At the end of the hallway was another, smaller red door that read "Mrs. Selway's Kindergarten Room" in yellow bubble letters. Standing at the door was a short, round, older woman with silver hair.

"You must be Henry!" she said. He looked back at his mom. As she nudged him forward, Mrs. Selway opened the door, and Henry saw something he couldn't believe. Dozens of kids were playing, laughing, and having a great time! Suddenly, Henry was a little excited. After hugging his mom, he turned around and ran straight into the classroom thinking, "Maybe this won't be so bad after all."

Strategy
When explaining an event or describing a character in the story, use details that are written in the story.

Test Tip
Look at the characters' words and actions to determine their feelings.

1. **How do you think Henry was feeling on his first day of kindergarten?**

   (A) excited

   (B) sleepy

   (C) nervous

   (D) sick

   What details from the story support your inference?

   _____

   _____

2. **What does the word *comforting* mean in the story?**

   (A) make something softer

   (B) make someone feel better

   (C) make someone nervous

   (D) make something louder

   Write how you know.

   _____

   _____

   _____

   _____

   _____

Name _____ Date _____

English Language Arts

Determine Theme and Summarize Text
Reading: Literature

DIRECTIONS: Read the story. Then, answer the questions.

> Maggie and Isabel went to the park on Saturday. They headed for the slides. However, they couldn't decide who should go first. Isabel said she should go first because she was older. Maggie said she should go first because Isabel was always first. Just then, their mother came over and said, "Why don't you each get on one slide and start down at the same time?" That's just what they did.

Strategy   Use ideas, events, and details from a story to determine its theme.

Test Tip   Find a story's theme by looking for details that tell what a major character learns during the story.

1. **What is this story about?**

   (A) a problem that is solved

   (B) an argument at the park

   (C) sisters who get along well

   (D) brothers who lost their dog

   What details helped you determine what the story is about?

   _____

   _____

   _____

   _____

2. **Who solves the problem in the story?**

   (A) the coach

   (B) Maggie

   (C) Isabel

   (D) the mother

3. **What was the problem in the story?**

   _____

   _____

4. **What was the solution to the problem?**

   _____

   _____

5. **Using details from the story, which theme best fits the story?**

   (A) If you can't agree, keep talking until you do.

   (B) Always tell people how you feel.

   (C) Try looking for a new solution if you can't agree.

   (D) Other people can help you solve problems.

   Write how you know.

   _____

   _____

6. **Write a summary of the story.**

   _____

   _____

   _____

   _____

   _____

Name _____ Date _____

Determine Theme and Summarize Text
Reading: Literature

DIRECTIONS: Read the story. Then, answer the questions.

Joel's hockey team had played well all season, and this was their chance to win the tournament. He was the best player.

He glanced around at his teammates. "Guys," he said, "let's skate really hard and show them how great we are!"

The team cheered and started to walk out to the ice. Joel turned around to grab his helmet, but it wasn't there. He looked under the benches and in the lockers, but his helmet wasn't anywhere. He sat down and felt his throat get tight. If he didn't have a helmet, he couldn't play.

Just then, there was a knock on the door. Joel's mom peeked her head around the locker room door. "Thank goodness," she said. "I got here just in time with your helmet."

Strategy   To discover the theme, ask yourself what the overall lesson or message of the passage is.

1. What is this story about?

   (A) a problem that is solved

   (B) an argument that is solved

   (C) a hockey team trying to win

   (D) hockey equipment

2. Who solves the problem in the story?

   (A) the coach

   (B) Joel

   (C) Joel's teammates

   (D) the mother

3. What was the problem in the story?

   _____

   _____

4. Which theme fits the story best?

   (A) Play hard and you will win.

   (B) Don't lose important things.

   (C) People close to you will help you.

   (D) Remember that it's only a game.

Write how you know.

_____

_____

_____

_____

5. If the story on page 9 and on this page appeared together in a book of similar stories, a good title for the book would be _____.

   (A) *Sports Bloopers*

   (B) *Mom to the Rescue*

   (C) *Sisters Who Argue*

   (D) *How to Play Hockey Without a Helmet*

English Language Arts

Determine the Meaning of Words and Phrases in a Text
Reading: Literature

DIRECTIONS: Read the story. Then, answer the questions.

> A percussionist, someone who plays a lots of instruments, came to my school today. His name is Marco.
>
> Marco said that by participating, or taking part, in the arts, you are helping your brain develop. This means that music, literature, and theater make you smarter! He told us about percussion and all of the different instruments he plays. One kind of instrument is a keyboard instrument, like the xylophone or marimba.
>
> Another instrument he told us about is the timpani. Timpani are big round drums. All you need to make them change pitch is a little foot pedal, almost like a gas pedal, at the bottom of the drum.
>
> He also told us about auxiliary instruments. Triangles, wood blocks, and maracas all are considered auxiliary, which means they are support instruments. These instruments are mostly for effect to help set a mood for different songs.
>
> The last kind of percussion instrument Marco told us about was hand drums. Bongos and congas are both types of hand drums, along with more eccentric, or rare, drums like the cahone and djembe.
>
> Thanks to Marco, I know a lot more about percussion and the arts than I did this morning, and I'm even thinking about trying music myself. It's cool to see how many instruments there are and how they can benefit, or help, you!

Strategy
While reading, identify word clues in a story to see how ideas are related and to determine word meanings.

Test Tip
The author doesn't always tell you what new words mean. You can use the context and what you already know to find the meanings.

1. **Which three following instruments belong in the percussion family?**

   (A) drums

   (B) timpani

   (C) guitar

   (D) triangle

2. **What are auxiliary instruments?**

   _____

   _____

3. **If you *participate* in an activity, what are you doing?**

   (A) quitting the activity

   (B) taking part in the activity

   (C) watching an activity

   (D) referring to an activity

   Which words in the story helped you with your answer?

   _____

4. **What is a synonym for *eccentric*?**

   _____

Name _____ Date _____

Determine the Meaning of Words and Phrases in a Text
Reading: Literature

DIRECTIONS: Read the story. Then, answer the questions.

"Daddy, Daddy!" Sarah shouted, as she entered the kitchen carefully carrying the fragile glass jar in her hands. It was dusk, and the sun was almost completely set. Sarah's dad turned from the sink to greet her, only to find a large glass jar of fireflies thrust into his face. "Look, look!"

Calmly, Sarah's dad examined the jar of illuminating bugs. "Isn't it cool how they light up like that?" Sarah exclaimed. "It is!" her father replied. "Every time they light up like that, they are actually taking a big gulp of oxygen, or air. It's how they breathe! When the light goes out, they're all out of breath."

"If they can't breathe anymore, they will die. But, we can help them live longer if we keep them out of the jar and in the backyard. There's more oxygen out there than there is in that jar," her dad said, smiling.

Shocked, Sarah immediately ran outside, only to return with a sad face and an empty jar. She began to cry, so her dad asked what was wrong. "I miss them!" Sarah exclaimed.

Taking Sarah's hand, her dad led her outside to the moon rising and the fireflies floating in and out of sight. "We can still see them, silly! We can even see more of them. Don't cry. You're helping them live longer, happier lives."

Maybe Sarah's dad was right. They looked a lot prettier floating around in the grass than a jar, anyway.

Strategy

Try replacing an unknown word with different meanings to see if that meaning makes sense in the sentence.

1. What does the word *illuminating* mean?

   (A) flying

   (B) shining

   (C) sleeping

   (D) eating

   Write how you know.

   _____

   _____

2. Why do fireflies need oxygen?

   _____

   _____

3. What time of day is *dusk*?

   (A) early morning

   (B) mid-afternoon

   (C) early evening

   (D) late night

   Which words from the story helped you answer?

   _____

   _____

4. How did Sarah's father convince Sarah to let the fireflies out of the jar?

   _____

   _____

English Language Arts

Describe Characters, Settings, and Events
Reading: Literature

DIRECTIONS: Read the story. Then, answer the questions.

THE FOX AND THE GRAPES

One warm summer day, a fox was walking along when he noticed a bunch of grapes on a vine above him. Cool, juicy grapes would taste so good. The more he thought about it, the more the fox wanted those grapes. He tried standing on his tiptoes. He tried jumping high in the air. He tried getting a running start before he jumped. But, no matter what he tried, the fox could not reach the grapes. As he angrily walked away, the fox muttered, "They were probably sour, anyway!"

MORAL: A person (or fox) sometimes pretends he or she does not want something he or she cannot have.

Strategy As you read, pick out specific details from the story to describe the setting, characters, and events.

Test Tip Use a character's words and actions to understand the reasons behind them.

1. **Describe the setting of the fable.**

   _____

   _____

2. **Why did the fox want the grapes so badly?**

   Ⓐ He was warm and thirsty.

   Ⓑ He was hungry.

   Ⓒ He didn't want anyone else to get them.

   Ⓓ He wanted to make grape jelly.

3. **The fox was very determined to get the grapes. What details in the story help you understand what the word *determined* means?**

   _____

   _____

   _____

4. **What detail supports the moral, "A person (or fox) sometimes pretends that he or she does not want something he or she cannot have."**

   Ⓐ "The more he thought about it, the more the fox wanted those grapes."

   Ⓑ "He tried standing on his tiptoes."

   Ⓒ "But, no matter what he tried, the fox could not reach the grapes."

   Ⓓ "As he angrily walked away, the fox muttered, 'They were probably sour anyway!'"

5. **Describe the character of fox using details from the story.**

   _____

   _____

   _____

   _____

   _____

   _____

Test Tip

A moral is a lesson that fables teach on how you should or should not act.

English Language Arts

Describe Characters, Settings, and Events
Reading: Literature

DIRECTIONS: Read the story. Then, answer the questions.

It was Friday, and school had just ended. Maria stepped off the bus and began to walk home. As she approached her front yard, she noticed something different. There was barking coming from the backyard. "What could that be?" thought Maria. "We don't have a dog."

However, when she walked into her backyard, she found just that. A dog!

"Woof, woof, woof!" it greeted her with its tail wagging. "Surprise!" Maria's parents yelled. "We got you a puppy. His name is Spot." Maria let out a squeak in surprise and jumped into the air. "I can't believe it!" she shouted.

Maria and Spot began to run to each other until he jumped up and rolled onto the ground. Maria giggled, and Spot licked her face. "Do you want to take him for a walk?" Maria's father asked. Maria nodded her head with a big grin on her face.

Her dad showed her how to put on Spot's leash, and they all went to the front yard to walk Spot. He pulled and tugged, but after a while, he began to walk with Maria. It made her happy. While they walked, Maria's dad told her about all of the responsibilities of owning a dog. "I promise to take care of him," she said.

When they got home, Maria sat in the backyard with Spot and fed him dog treats. He wagged his tail and licked his lips. Then, he flopped over so Maria could rub his belly. Maria patted him gently, smiling the whole time. Over and over, she told herself how happy she was.

When her dad called her to come in for bed, Maria got up and Spot followed. Before they got inside, she whispered, "I love you, Spot." Spot let out a soft "woof," and they walked in together.

Strategy   As you read, ask yourself *Who? What? Where? When? How?* and *Why?* Use the answers to find details about characters, settings, and events.

Test Tip   The setting of a story is not only where the story happens, but also when it happens.

1. **Describe the setting of this story. Use details from the story.**

_____

_____

2. **Do you think Maria is a responsible girl? Explain your answer.**

_____

_____

_____

3. **How does Maria feel about getting a new puppy?**

  (A) upset

  (B) overwhelmed

  (C) scared

  (D) excited

Write how you know.

_____

_____

_____

Explain Differences Between Poetry, Drama, and Prose

Reading: Literature

DIRECTIONS: Read the poem. Then, answer the questions.

BACKPACK

My backpack's so heavy
It must weigh a ton.
With thousands of books—
My work's never done.

My arms are so sore
I can't lift a pen.
My breath is so short
I need oxygen.

When I stoop over,
it makes me fall down.
I think I'll just stay here
All squashed on the ground.

Strategy
Learn which elements, or features, are part of poems, stories, and plays. Use these features to identify the genre you are reading and to understand why words, phrases, and sentences are organized in a certain way.

Test Tip
Poems use rhyme and rhythm as well as colorful language. Poems are organized by stanza instead of by paragraph and by line instead of by sentence.

1. **Who do you think the speaker, or narrator, of the poem is?**
   - (A) a coach
   - (B) a student
   - (C) a swimmer
   - (D) a parent

   Write how you know.

   _____

   _____

   _____

2. **What might have led to the poet writing this poem?**
   - (A) a sale on backpacks that hold many books
   - (B) a student complaining about too much homework
   - (C) a child complaining about a heavy backpack
   - (D) a dog running away with a child's backpack

3. **Summarize this poem in a sentence.**

   _____

   _____

4. **In which stanzas does the narrator describe the effects of having a heavy backpack?**
   - (A) Stanzas 1 and 2
   - (B) Stanzas 2 and 3
   - (C) Stanzas 1 and 3
   - (D) Stanzas 1, 2, and 3

5. **How is this poem different from a story about a backpack?**

   _____

   _____

   _____

Explain Differences Between Poetry, Drama, and Prose

Reading: Literature

DIRECTIONS: Read the poem. Then, answer the questions.

POLAR BEARS

With fur like a snowstorm
And eyes like the night,
Two giant old bears
Sure gave me a fright.

They came up behind me
As quiet as mice,
And tapped on my shoulder.
Their paws were like ice.

As high as a kite,
I jumped in the air,
And turned round to see
Those bears standing there.

"We're sorry we scared you,"
The bears said so cool.
"We just came to ask you
To fill up our pool!"

Strategy — While reading, identify the meaning of figurative language, and use the meaning to understand a poem or story.

Test Tip — Figurative language includes words and phrases that have meanings beyond their literal meanings. Figurative language is language used for descriptive effect. Similes use *like* or *as* to compare things that may seem different.

1. Which two elements would be used if this poem were written as a story?

Ⓐ sentences and paragraphs

Ⓑ no rhyming words

Ⓒ no figurative language

Ⓓ stanzas and lines

2. How does the poem use rhyme?

_____

_____

_____

DIRECTIONS: Fill in the blanks to complete the similes from the poem. Then, write what each simile means on the line.

3. fur like _____

This means: _____

4. eyes like _____

This means: _____

5. as quiet as _____

This means: _____

_____

6. as high as _____

This means:_____

7. Rewrite Stanza 3 using sentences without figurative language.

_____

_____

_____

_____

Explain Differences Between Poetry, Drama, and Prose
Reading: Literature

DIRECTIONS: Read the play. Then, answer the questions.

Act 1, Scene 1
A cold winter's day, out in the snowy backyard of John's house.

John is standing in his yard. He is watching some geese fly overhead. Suddenly, a large, white paw can be seen tapping his left shoulder.
John (smiling, turning around): Yes?
Bear #1 and Bear #2 stand behind John.
As John's visitors come fully into view, John jumps into the air with a shriek.
Bear #1: Oh, we are so sorry. We didn't mean to scare you.
John: You are talking to me.
Bear #2: Well, yes, sir. We are talking to you. We were wondering . . .
John cuts him off.
John: Wait a minute! You are polar bears. You have white fur and black eyes. Your paws are freezing cold. I know I'm awake. But, you're talking to me.
Bear #1 to Bear #2: This may take a while.
The bears sit on their haunches, waiting.
John (to himself): Bears. Are talking. To me.
Finally, John shakes his head and walks toward the fence.
Bear #2 to Bear #1: We can wait.

Act 1, Scene 2
John's backyard. The bears are still sitting patiently. John is muttering to himself by the fence.
John (returning to the bears): Okay. So, you're talking polar bears. I can deal with that.
The bears stand up. John takes a step backward.
Bear #1 (to John): Are you going to be all right?
John (stammering): Yes, I think so. Ahem, so what can I do for you two gentle—, um, bears?
Bear #2: We were just wondering if you could fill our pool for us.
John looks from Bear #2 to Bear #1. They watch him expectantly.
John (shrugging): Polar bears are asking me to fill their pool. Ok, why not? Lead the way.
John and bears walk off stage right.
End Scene

English Language Arts

Explain Differences Between Poetry, Drama, and Prose
Reading: Literature

Strategy Compare a poem, story, and play and identify how they have different structures, or formats.

Test Tip A play uses stage directions to tell what characters do, how they move, and how they speak. The dialogue appears after the speaker's name.

1. What is the setting of Act 1, Scene 1?

_____

_____

2. How do the stage directions help you visualize the action in the play?

_____

_____

_____

_____

3. How is the play similar to the poem on the previous page?

(A) They both have talking polar bears.

(B) They both have a character named John.

(C) They both take place in the summer.

(D) They both give details about the setting.

4. In which scene does John learn why the polar bears are in his yard?

_____

5. Compare the play to a poem and story. Note the elements or formats of each type of writing and tell what is different.

_____

_____

_____

_____

_____

_____

Name _____ Date _____

English Language Arts

Compare and Contrast Different Points of View
Reading: Literature

DIRECTIONS: Read the stories.

A DAY AT THE BEACH

Today, Sam visited the ocean for the very first time. "You'll love it," his mom told him along the way. He was very excited. What would it be like? Would it smell different from other places? Would it be warmer or colder? Would it be okay to swim in the ocean, or would a shark eat him? These were all questions, and he needed answers.

When they arrived at the ocean, Sam was amazed. It did smell different! Sam's mom told him that was because of all the salt in the water. It was cooler! Sam's mom told him that was because of the breeze coming off the ocean. Most importantly, though, it was okay to swim in the ocean. Even if it was a little chilly. "And no," Sam's mom told him, "a shark will not eat you. They're just as scared of you as you are of them!"

Sam and his mom spent the day walking on the beach and putting their toes in the water. They even swam for a while, and Sam could swear he saw some turtles. They went to a restaurant and ate sea salt fries. Then, they got ice cream and took lots of silly pictures.

Sam decided he liked the beach. Sam's mom told him she knew he would love it. "The beach is my favorite place. But, I guess I will share it with you!" she said while she laughed. He grinned, and they got in the car but not until they shook the sand from their shoes.

I LIKE TO RUN!

My name is Maya, and I like to run. There is no better feeling than the wind on my face and the road beneath my feet. When I run, I feel like I am flying.

Running is important. When I was little, running was always my favorite kind of exercise. I would run in races against boys and beat them. I would run in games, like tag and kickball. I would run in circles in my backyard with my dog. I would find any reason to run. Running made me feel special. Running still makes me feel that way.

As I got older, I started running on sports teams, like soccer and track. Everyone told me I was really good at it. All of their kind words made me want to work harder so I could be even better. I practiced every day. Sometimes, I would run for short distances as fast as I could. Other times, I liked to run for a long time and go nice and slow.

One day, I want to run as fast as Usain Bolt. He is the fastest man alive. He is also my hero. I know if I work hard, I might be able to make it one day. If I keep putting my mind to it, I can do it. I can do anything.

English Language Arts
Compare and Contrast Different Points of View
Reading: Literature

DIRECTIONS: Use the stories to answer the questions.

Strategy | While reading, identify who the narrator is in the story to understand the point of view.

Test Tip | A story with first-person point of view has a narrator that is a character in the story. The narrator uses "I" and reveals his or her thoughts. A story with third-person point of view has a narrator that is not part of the story.

1. **From whose point of view is each story written?**

   A Day at the Beach: _____

   I Like to Run!: _____

   Write how you know.

   _____

   _____

   _____

2. **In the story "A Day at the Beach," how does the narrator show how Sam is feeling?**

   _____

   _____

3. **In which story does the reader learn from the character exactly how they are feeling?**

   _____

4. **Why is it easier to know exactly how a character feels when the story is told from the character's point of view, rather than when it is told from a narrator's point of view?**

   (A) The character tells you exactly what he or she is feeling.

   (B) The narrator describes what the character does.

   (C) The character tells about what he or she does.

   (D) The narrator tells what the character says.

5. **How did Sam feel about going to the ocean? Choose all that apply.**

   (A) He was excited.

   (B) He had many questions.

   (C) He didn't want to go.

   (D) He had been there a thousand times.

6. **Is there a way to know how the characters in "A Day at the Beach" felt at the end of the story? Write how you know.**

   _____

   _____

7. **What is another way Maya could have said, "run short distances as fast as I can"?**

   (A) jog

   (B) rush

   (C) sprint

   (D) stroll

8. **What is another way the narrator could have said, "putting their toes in the water"?**

   (A) splashing in the water

   (B) jumping in the water

   (C) wading in the water

   (D) dipping their toes in the water

Name _____ Date _____

English Language Arts

Compare and Contrast Different Points of View
Reading: Literature

Strategy To figure out the point of view, ask yourself *Who is telling the story? What do they know?*

Test Tip Stories with third-person point of view have narrators that know what events are happening. They may know what characters are thinking and feeling.

DIRECTIONS: For each sentence, write if the point of view is *first person* or *third person*.

9. I was so excited to see the ocean!

_____

10. "Dad," said Maya, "I'm going out running."

_____

11. Sam couldn't wait to get to the beach.

_____

12. I am going to train for a marathon.

_____

DIRECTIONS: Rewrite each sentence in the opposite point of view. If the sentence is written in third person, rewrite it in first person. If the sentence is written in first person, rewrite it in third person.

13. Today, Sam visited the ocean for the very first time.

_____

_____

_____

14. My name is Maya, and I like to run.

_____

_____

15. Sam and his mom spent the day walking on the beach and putting their toes in the water.

_____

_____

_____

_____

16. One day, I want to run as fast as Usain Bolt.

_____

_____

_____

Compare and Contrast Stories
Reading: Literature

DIRECTIONS: Read the story. Then, answer the questions.

ADAPTED FROM "JASON AND THE GOLDEN FLEECE"

Jason was the son of the king, but his uncle had stolen the throne. His uncle lived in constant fear of losing what he had taken. He kept Jason's father prisoner and would have murdered Jason at birth. But, Jason's mother tricked him by acting as if Jason had died. Meanwhile, the infant was sent to be raised by Chiron the Centaur.

When Jason was old enough, he returned to the kingdom to claim the throne. But, his uncle had no intention of giving it up, especially to a stranger. He invited Jason to a banquet. During the meal, he said to Jason, "You may rule the kingdom if you bring back the Golden Fleece. It's a quest that any hero worth his salt would leap at."

Jason and his crew encountered many dangers on their journey. Each time, a kind stranger came to help the heroes avoid harm.

Once he arrived in the kingdom where the Golden Fleece was kept, Jason had to face a series of challenges from its king. The king considered the Golden Fleece his own. The king's daughter, Medea, reminded him to be kind. Medea quietly offered to help Jason. She helped him accomplish all of his challenges

However, the king told Medea that he would never give the Fleece to Jason. Medea told this to Jason. She offered to lead him to the temple grove where the Fleece was nailed to a tree and guarded by a dragon. So, at midnight, they crept into the grove. Jason, ever the hothead, whipped out his sword, but Medea wisely held his arm.

Instead, she used a sleeping potion on the monster. Together, they made off with the Fleece and escaped to the ship. Setting sail at once, they escaped. Thus, Jason succeeded in his heroic challenge.

Strategy

Determine a story's theme by identifying the main character, the main character's problem, and how the problem is solved.

Test Tip

A theme is the overall idea or message in the story. A myth is a traditional tale that usually involves supernatural elements. Myths are usually about heroes on quests, which are adventures that require them to accomplish a dangerous task.

1. Who is the hero in this myth?

Ⓐ the uncle

Ⓑ Jason

Ⓒ Medea

Ⓓ the king

Write how you know.

_____

2. Describe the character of Jason. Use details from the story.

_____

_____

_____

_____

Name _____   Date _____

English Language Arts

Compare and Contrast Stories
Reading: Literature

DIRECTIONS: Use the story to answer the questions.

Strategy   Review the characters in the story and the plot. Use what happens to each character and how they respond to identify the theme of the story.

Test Tip   Look for patterns in a story, or details that seem to repeat. If an idea is presented many times, it is related to the story's theme.

3. Describe Jason's uncle. Use details from the story.

_____

_____

_____

_____

4. Why did Jason agree to go on the quest?

_____

_____

Write how you know.

_____

_____

_____

5. Why does Jason's uncle send him on the quest to get the Golden Fleece?

(A) He needs the Golden Fleece to keep the throne.

(B) He knows it is very dangerous and Jason might not succeed.

(C) He wants Jason to prove he is worthy of the throne.

(D) He thinks Jason will refuse to go on the quest.

Write how you know.

_____

_____

6. Why did Medea help Jason take the Golden Fleece from her father?

_____

_____

7. Do you think Jason would have succeeded on his quest without the help of others? Explain.

_____

_____

_____

8. Which sentence best describes the theme of the story?

(A) Strength is better than kindness.

(B) Challenges are difficult to face.

(C) Heroes can do everything on their own.

(D) Everyone needs help at some point.

Write how you know.

_____

_____

_____

_____

English Language Arts

Compare and Contrast Stories
Reading: Literature

DIRECTIONS: Read the story. Then, answer the questions.

ADAPTED FROM THE STORY OF RAMA AND SITA

A good man, called Rama, was married to a beautiful princess, called Sita. Prince Rama was the son of a great King and was expected to become King himself one day. However, his stepmother wanted her son to become King. She tricked her husband into banishing Rama and his wife Sita to live in the forest with his brother, Lakshman.

But, this was no ordinary forest. This was the forest where demons lived, including Demon King Ravana. Ravana had 20 arms and 10 heads. There were 2 eyes on each head and a row of sharp yellow teeth. When Ravana saw Sita, he wanted her for himself. He decided to kidnap her. When Rama was out of sight, Ravana disguised himself as an old man and tricked Sita. He flew off with Sita in a chariot pulled by flying monsters.

Sita was afraid, but she was also clever. Being a princess, she wore jewelry, and she dropped her jewels, piece by piece, onto the ground to leave a trail for Rama. Rama, realizing he had been tricked, discovered the trail. He also came upon his friend Hanuman, King of the Monkeys. Hanuman promised Rama he and all the monkeys would help Rama find Sita, and they searched the world looking for her. Eventually, a monkey located Sita on a dark, isolated island surrounded by rocks and stormy seas. Hanuman flew to Sita. She gave him her last precious pearl to give to Rama and prove it was really her. She had been found! The monkeys helped Rama for a second time by throwing stones and rocks into the sea until they had built a great bridge to the island.

Hanuman, Rama, and Lakshman prepared for battle. This was one of the greatest battles ever seen. The fighting lasted for 10 days. It looked as though Ravana was going to win, until Rama borrowed a special bow and arrow from the gods. Rama shot Ravana through the heart, and the battle was won. Rama rescued Sita, and they returned home. As it got dark, the people of the kingdom put out little oil lamps in their windows to show the way home. Everyone was happy, and Rama and Sita ruled well.

Strategy
Compare the themes in different stories, looking for how they are similar.

1. Why were Rama and Sita banished to the forest?

(A) Rama gave up his title of prince.

(B) Sita was found to be an evil sorceress.

(C) Rama's stepmother wanted her son to be king.

(D) Rama's father didn't want to give up his kingdom.

Write how you know.

_____

_____

2. Write two details from the story that describe the setting.

_____

_____

3. Why did Prince Rama's stepmother choose to banish Rama and Sita to this forest?

(A) Rama would enjoy living in the forest.

(B) Sita was afraid of forest animals.

(C) The forest was far away from the castle.

(D) Ravana lived there and would harm them.

Compare and Contrast Stories
Reading: Literature

DIRECTIONS: Use the story to answer the questions.

Strategy — Compare themes by looking for similarities in characters, events, and ideas.

4. **What detail shows that Sita was clever?**

_____

_____

_____

_____

5. **Who helped Rama fight Ravana? Choose all that apply.**

(A) his stepmother

(B) the king of the monkeys

(C) the king of the demons

(D) his uncle, Lakshman

6. **What are two similarities between this myth and the myth of "Jason and the Golden Fleece"?**

_____

_____

_____

_____

Write how you know.

_____

_____

_____

_____

7. **What are two differences between the myths?**

_____

_____

_____

_____

8. **Which theme applies to both stories?**

(A) Family is the most important thing in life.

(B) With help from others, you can overcome challenges.

(C) People who want power will always win.

(D) Heroes are easily tricked by magic.

Write how you know.

_____

_____

_____

_____

_____

9. **Which patterns are present in both myths? Look for ideas or events that appear in each story.**

_____

_____

_____

_____

English Language Arts

Explain and Support Inferences
Reading: Informational Text

DIRECTIONS: Read the passage. Then answer the questions.

Have you ever seen someone send a code for SOS? Maybe you've seen an old movie showing a ship about to sink. Perhaps, someone on the ship was tapping wildly on a device. That person was using the telegraph to send for help. Samuel Morse invented the telegraph. He also invented the electronic alphabet called *Morse Code*. The code is a set of dots and dashes that stand for each number and letter of the alphabet.

In 1832, Morse was sailing back to the United States from Europe. During the trip, he came up with the idea of an electronic telegraph. It would help people communicate across great distances. They could be in contact with each other from ship to shore. He was eager to make his invention as quickly as possible.

By 1835, he had made his first telegraph. However, it was only a trial version. In 1844, he built a telegraph line. It went from Baltimore to Washington, D.C. The telegraph line was like a telephone line today. It carried Morse Code messages from one person to another. Morse kept working to make his telegraph better. In 1849, the government gave him a patent. This gave him the right to make his invention. Within a few years, there were 23,000 miles of telegraph wire. People could now communicate across great distances. As a result of his invention, trains ran more safely. Conductors could warn about dangers or problems and ask for help. People in businesses could communicate more easily. This made it easier to sell their goods and services. Morse had changed communication forever.

Strategy — Explain the passage and infer by using words and phrases exactly as they appear in the passage.

Test Tip — The main idea is what the passage is *mostly* about. Details tell more about the main idea.

1. What is the main idea of this passage?

_____

_____

2. What details helped you answer question 1?

_____

_____

_____

_____

_____

3. What word parts make the word *telegraph*?

_____ and _____

4. Write three words using the word part *tele-*.

_____

_____

_____

5. What is *Morse Code*?

(A) a set of bumps used to help blind people read

(B) a set of dots and dashes that stand for letters and numbers

(C) a secret code used by the FBI

(D) the password for an e-mail account

English Language Arts

Explain and Support Inferences
Reading: Informational Text

DIRECTIONS: Read the passage. Then, answer the questions.

Perhaps you have heard that many types of bats have very small eyes and do not see well. Still, as they swoop through the night, they do not bump into objects and are able to find food, even though they can't see their prey. How is this possible? Echolocation.

You might recognize the beginning of the word *echolocation* as *echo*, and you might recognize the last part of the word as *location*. This gives you clues about how echolocation works. The bat sends out sounds. The sounds bounce off objects and return to the bat. Echolocation not only tells the bat that objects are nearby, but it also tells the bat just how far away the objects are.

Bats are not the only creatures that use echolocation. Porpoises and some types of whales and birds also use it. It is a very effective tool for the animals that use it.

Strategy As you read a passage, make inferences by using what you know from the text and what you know from your own experiences or other stories you have read.

Test Tip An inference must be supported by details in the text.

1. What is the main idea of this passage?

_____

_____

_____

Write how you know.

_____

_____

_____

2. Why are the details about bats having very small eyes and not seeing well important?

   (A) to explain why bats are up at night

   (B) to describe what bats look like

   (C) to show why they use echolocation

   (D) to prove that bats are blind

Write how you know.

_____

_____

3. Why do you think the writer chose to show how *echolocation* can be broken into *echo* and *location*?

_____

_____

4. Why do animals use echolocation? Choose all that apply.

   (A) to keep from bumping into things at night

   (B) to locate prey they can't see

   (C) to tell the distance of an object

   (D) to hear the sound of its own voice

English Language Arts

Determine the Theme and Summarize Text
Reading: Informational Text

DIRECTIONS: Read the passage. Then, answer the questions.

> Mars is about 225 million kilometers away from Earth. But, in terms of similarities, Mars is the closest planet to Earth.
>
> Mars is named after the Roman god of war. It is the fourth planet from the sun and is the second smallest planet in our solar system, after Mercury. It is often described as the "Red Planet." Mars is called the Red Planet because of large amounts of iron oxide on its surface. Iron oxide is a chemical that gives Mars its red color. Other colors seen on the surface of Mars are gold, brown, tan, and green. Each color is a result of different elements on the surface of Mars.
>
> The United States has attempted 39 missions to Mars. Of these, only 16 have been successful. Five different spacecraft are currently observing Mars. Three of these craft are in orbit around Mars. The other two are on the surface. These spacecraft study the surface of Mars and send back information for scientists to examine. They have found that many of the features of Mars are similar to those of Earth.
>
> Aside from iron oxide, there are many other elements and rocks on Mars, making it a terrestrial planet. A terrestrial planet is one that has a hard surface, like Earth. Mars also has many surface features similar to both Earth and the moon. It has impact craters like the moon and valleys, deserts, and polar ice caps like Earth. The largest mountain in the solar system is found on Mars. Also, Mars has the largest dust storms in the universe.
>
> Mars is approximately half the size of Earth and is less dense. Mars has about 15% of Earth's volume and 11% of its mass. The total surface area of Mars is almost equal to the total area of dry land on Earth. Although Mars is larger and more massive than Mercury, Mercury is denser. For this reason, both planets have a similar gravitational pull at their surface. The gravity on Mars is only about 38% of the gravity on Earth. So, if you weigh 100 pounds on Earth, you would only weigh 38 pounds on the surface of Mars!
>
> Because Mars is the planet most similar to Earth, scientists are searching for signs of life. So far, they have found evidence of water on Mars. This discovery is an important step in learning more about the red planet.

Strategy   Identify a main idea for each paragraph of an informational passage. Then, find details that support the main ideas.

Test Tip   A main idea is not the topic of the passage. It is what the passage is mostly, or mainly, about.

English Language Arts

Determine the Theme and Summarize Text
Reading: Informational Text

1. What is the main idea of this passage?

(A) Mars is far away from Earth.

(B) Mars has the largest mountain in the solar system.

(C) Mars is the planet most similar to Earth.

(D) There have only been 16 successful missions to Mars.

2. Write three details that support the main idea.

_____

_____

_____

_____

_____

_____

3. Why do scientists study Mars?

(A) They are looking for Martians.

(B) They are searching for signs of life.

(C) They are hoping to move people there soon.

(D) They need to find more water for Earth.

4. How is Mars different from Earth?

_____

_____

_____

_____

5. Write three things you learned about Mars from this passage.

_____

_____

_____

_____

_____

_____

_____

6. What would you look for to write a summary of the passage?

_____

_____

_____

_____

_____

_____

English Language Arts
Determine the Theme and Summarize Text
Reading: Informational Text

DIRECTIONS: Read the passage. Then, answer the questions.

Go to an aquarium, or even a pet store, and you can see hundreds of beautiful sea creatures. From rainbow-colored fish to coral, these animals are undeniably beautiful. But, there are other creatures in the Earth's seas that most people would not consider beautiful. In fact, they might consider them downright weird.

The blobfish has been voted the world's ugliest creature. A part of the group of fishes called "fatheads," the blobfish is a deep-water fish that lives off the coast of Australia. It has pale, jelly-like flesh with loose skin, beady, staring eyes, and a big nose. The blobfish floats above the floor of the ocean not really spending much energy. While nobody has ever seen a blobfish eat, scientists believe they likely open their mouths and eat whatever happens to float in.

The Dana octopus squid is another weird sea creature. It is one of the largest squid species and can grow up to 7.5 feet long. The Dana octopus squid sends off flashes of bright light from its tentacles as it attacks its prey. Scientists believe the squid uses these bright flashes of light to confuse its prey. The flashes may also be used as a sort of flashlight, lighting up the prey so the squid can capture it. Young Dana octopus squid have also been seen swimming toward predators flashing their lights, perhaps to confuse them and allow other squid to escape.

One last weird sea creature is the viperfish. This fish is most known for its large predatory teeth and hinged lower jaw. The viperfish's fangs would not even fit in their mouth if they didn't curl up toward their eyes. Like the Dana octopus squid, the viperfish lights up. The light helps them catch prey and communicate to other viperfish. Viperfish grow to two feet long and can live up to 40 years!

There are thousands of species that call our oceans home. Many of them are beautiful, and just as many are unusual.

Strategy
Summarize a passage in your own words using the main ideas to make sure you understand it.

1. What is the main idea of this passage?

(A) There are many beautiful fish in the oceans.

(B) Viperfish have a very weird appearance.

(C) There are many unusual creatures in the oceans.

(D) The blobfish was voted the world's ugliest creature.

Write how you know.

_____

_____

_____

2. Three examples of weird sea creatures are featured in this passage. Write three details about each that support the main idea.

Blobfish:

_____

_____

Dana octopus squid:

_____

_____

Viperfish:

_____

_____

English Language Arts

Explain Historical, Scientific, and Technical Text

Reading: Informational Text

DIRECTIONS: Read the passage. Then, answer the questions.

> In 1908, Jacqueline Cochran was born to a poor family in Florida. Like many girls at the time, she went to work at an early age. When she was just 8 years old, she started work in a cotton mill. As she made cloth, she dreamed about becoming a pilot. She wanted to fly one of the recently invented planes.
>
> Jacqueline got her wish in the 1930s. At this time, only a few daring young men flew these new planes. There were few women pilots. That did not stop Jacqueline. She took flying lessons and became a pilot. She began to enter famous races. In 1938, she won first prize in a contest to fly across the United States.
>
> At the beginning of World War II, Jacqueline trained women in England as pilots. She later returned to the United States and trained American women, too. In 1945, she earned the Distinguished Service Medal. It is one of America's highest honors.
>
> When jet planes were invented, Jacqueline learned to fly them, too. She was the first woman to fly faster than the speed of sound. She also set many other records, including flying higher than anyone had before her.
>
> In many ways, Jacqueline is forgotten today. But, she was a pioneer in a new technology. She helped to make air travel one of our most important means of transportation.

Strategy Look for details that explain the type of information given in a text—historical, technical, or scientific. Then, use those details to explain the information.

Test Tip Biographies are historical passages because they tell about the history of someone's life. Look for time words and dates to help you sequence events in a person's life.

1. How was Jacqueline Cochran a pioneer in new technology?

_____

_____

_____

2. List five details that show that Jacqueline Cochran was a pioneer and explain the events in the passage.

_____

_____

_____

_____

3. Which words and phrases did the author use to order the events in the passage?

_____

_____

_____

4. How is this an example of historical text?

_____

_____

English Language Arts

Explain Historical, Scientific, and Technical Text
Reading: Informational Text

DIRECTIONS: Read the passage. Then, answer the questions.

THE NORTH STAR

The North Star is one of the most famous stars. Its star name is *Polaris*. It is called the North Star because it shines almost directly over the North Pole. If you are at the North Pole, the North Star is overhead. As you travel farther south, the star seems lower in the sky. Only people in the Northern Hemisphere can see the North Star.

Because the North Star is always in the same spot in the sky, it has served to give direction to people at night for years. Sailors used the North Star to navigate through the oceans.

Polaris, like all stars, is always moving. Thousands of years from now, another star will get to be the North Star. Vega was the North Star thousands of years before it moved out of position and Polaris became the North Star.

Strategy

Explain information in a passage by finding details in the passage, Then, be sure to use words and phrases from the passage in the explanation.

Test Tip

Scientific passages usually are written with a cause-effect structure. Look for words that show cause-and-effect relationships.

1. **The North Star might be one of the most famous stars because _____.**

   (A) it is near the North Pole

   (B) it is always moving

   (C) it is always in the same spot

   (D) it is difficult to find

2. **Why will another star get to be the North Star someday?**

   _____

   _____

3. **The name *Polaris* most likely comes from which name?**

   (A) polecat

   (B) polar bear

   (C) Poland

   (D) North Pole

Write how you know.

   _____

   _____

4. **Why do you think only people in the Northern Hemisphere can see the North Star?**

   _____

   _____

5. **Write a sentence from the passage that shows a cause-and-effect structure.**

   _____

   _____

   _____

   _____

   _____

English Language Arts

Describe the Overall Structure of a Text
Reading: Informational Text

DIRECTIONS: Read the passage. Then, answer the questions.

KELP FORESTS

Both rain forests and kelp forests are important to our ecology. They keep animals safe by providing homes. Rain forests keep land animals safe, whereas kelp forests keep sea creatures safe.

Like rain forests, kelp forests are homes for many types of creatures. Crab, eel, lobster, and seahorses are just a few of the sea creatures that live in sea kelp. In California, kelp forests are home to more than 770 sea species. A sandy ocean bottom can make a home for some creatures, but a kelp forest can make a home for thousands more.

Like a rain forest, a kelp forest has layers. You will find three main layers in a kelp forest. They are the canopy, middle, and floor layers. The canopy is at the top, and the floor is at the bottom.

You will find different sea creatures and plants at different levels. Herring and mackerel like to swim through the canopy. Sea slugs and snails feast on sea mats they find in the canopy.

Sea urchins look for food in the middle layer. Sea anemones, crabs, and lobsters live on the floor level. Older blue-rayed limpets feast here too.

Like a rain forest, a kelp forest is a complex habitat for many sea creatures. It keeps them safe from predators and people. To keep kelp forests an important part of our ecology, we must protect them from pollution and destruction.

Strategy   Identify passage structure by asking yourself if the passage compares, explains why, or presents two sides to an issue.

Test Tip   Passages that have a compare/contrast structure give information about how an idea or thing is the same and different.

1. **Which sentence describes the main idea of the passage?**

   Ⓐ A kelp forest has three levels.

   Ⓑ Rain forests and kelp forests help our ecology.

   Ⓒ Many sea creatures live in kelp forests and rain forests.

   Ⓓ Kelp forests are like rain forests.

   Write how you know.

   _____

   _____

   _____

2. **Which sentence is the main idea of Paragraph 3?**

   _____

   _____

3. **How would you describe the structure of this passage?**

   _____

4. **What words are clues about the structure of the passage?**

   _____

English Language Arts

Describe the Overall Structure of a Text
Reading: Informational Text

DIRECTIONS: Read the passage. Then, answer the questions.

It was 13 years ago, but I remember it as if it were yesterday: September 11, 2001. I was in my second-grade classroom. Students were in their reading groups. I had a group at the table reading with me. Another group was reading in a corner. I remember Kevin at the science table rubbing two rocks together to make dust. The sound was driving me crazy, but he was working intently, and I didn't want to interrupt him.

Suddenly, my door burst open and a parent volunteer rushed over to me.

"Did you hear? A plane crashed into the World Trade Center!" she whispered in my ear.

I didn't know what she was talking about, but soon I, along with everyone else in the world, would know exactly how this horrible tragedy unfolded.

For the next several days, there was nothing on television but news coverage of the disaster. It was all you could see in the newspapers, all you could hear on the radio. It was frightening. The most eerie part was the missing airplanes. I live between two major international airports, and the skies were silent. Never in my life had I experienced such a thing. Never had the world been so quiet.

Strategy Look for clue words to identify text structure: *first, then, next, finally.*

Test Tip Passages that use sequence structures often use words, dates, and phrases that tell when an event happened.

1. What is the structure of this story?

(A) problem/solution

(B) cause/effect

(C) chronology

(D) compare/contrast

Write how you know.

_____

_____

_____

_____

2. How would the passage be different if the author had used a cause-and-effect structure?

_____

_____

_____

_____

_____

Compare Two Texts
Reading: Informational Text

DIRECTIONS: Read each passage. Then, answer the questions on the next page.

FENCING

Fencing is the art of fighting with swords. The most common type of fencing today is called Olympic Fencing or competitive fencing. Fencing is one of only five sports that have appeared in every modern Olympic games.

The art of fencing is divided into 3 weapons categories: foil, saber, and épée. The foil is the most common weapon used in competition. There are electric foils and "dry" foils. The "dry" foil has a steel blade that is folded at the tip and capped. This prevents injury. The blade of a foil is made to bend when it strikes an opponent. The blade is no more than 90 centimeters long. In most competitions, including the Olympics, the electric foil is used.

The saber is a modern fencing weapon. The blade on an adult's saber is 88 centimeters long. At the end of the blade, the point is folded for safety. The saber is shorter than either the foil or épée, which makes it easier to move quickly. The electric saber was introduced in 1988.

An épée is the modern spin-off of the dueling sword. The word *épée* is French for *sword*. The épée is a thrusting sword that is similar in shape to the foil. However, the épée has a stiffer blade than the foil. The épée is the heaviest of the three fencing swords.

Fencing has been around since ancient times, but it has only been a competitive sport in modern times. Three types of swords are used, each with its own set of rules and regulations.

TYPE OF SWORD	MAXIMUM LENGTH OF BLADE	MAXIMUM WEIGHT	COMPETITIVE WEIGHT	SHAPE OF BLADE
Foil	90 cm	500 g	350 g	Rectangular
Saber	88 cm	500 g	400 g	y- or v-shaped
Épée	90 cm	770 g	300–450 g	Triangular

FENCING CLASS

When I get to my fencing class, the first thing I do is get my gear on. My gear includes a jacket, body wire, a mask, a glove, and an electric vest. I get my sword, and I'm ready for class.

The next thing I do is connect to the electric fencing machine. There is a wire that connects to my vest and sword. Then, it is connected to a machine that puts out a beep when someone scores. Most fencers in my class don't do this, but I'm in the advanced class. The next thing I do is wait for another person to get ready. When someone else is ready and connected, we start dueling.

The first person to get 5 points wins. To get points in fencing, you have to hit your opponent in certain areas. With a foil, you can hit only in the chest and stomach areas. With the saber, you get points for hitting anywhere on your opponent's upper body. With the épée, you can hit your opponent anywhere. Sometimes, it hurts a little when you get hit with one of the swords. There is under armor you can wear to make the strikes not hurt as much.

The loser of the match either sits or starts dueling someone else. Then, you play two games, and whether you win or lose them, you have to sit or duel someone else.

If you are a beginner, you put on your gear and wait for the instructor to be ready. Beginners do not use electric swords. Then, you do some footwork drills. After that, you sit and wait until it's your turn to duel. You do 2 rounds in a row, and then, you sit. After everyone competes in 4–6 rounds, you do a 3-weapon tournament. This is when someone goes to the fencing strip and someone else picks which of the 3 swords to use. Then, you duel, and the first person to 3 points wins and gets to stay for another round.

Compare Two Texts
Reading: Informational Text

Strategy Identify details from two passages on the same topic to combine the information and learn more about the topic.

Test Tip Each passage has details about the topic that are similar and details that are different. Putting all of the details together will help you know more about the topic.

1. **What is fencing?**

   _____

2. **Why are the tips of the foil and saber folded?**

   _____

   _____

3. **Write some ways that the 3 types of swords are different.**

   _____

   _____

   _____

4. **How does the table help you understand the information in the first passage?**

   (A) It organizes it so it is easy to read.

   (B) It gives new information.

   (C) It tells when each sword was invented.

   (D) It is a timeline of fencing history.

5. **What gear do advanced students use in fencing? Choose all that apply.**

   (A) jacket

   (B) glove

   (C) electric vest

   (D) boots

6. **Describe how a fencer earns points when using a foil.**

   _____

   _____

7. **How are the two passages about fencing different?**

   _____

   _____

   _____

   _____

   _____

8. **How does reading the first passage help you better understand the second passage?**

   _____

   _____

   _____

   _____

   _____

   _____

Compare Two Texts
Reading: Informational Text

DIRECTIONS: Read each passage. Then, answer the questions on the next page.

MARTIN LUTHER KING, JR.

Martin Luther King, Jr. was born Michael King on January 15, 1929. He was born in Atlanta, Georgia. His parents were the Reverend Michael King, Sr., and Alberta Williams King. Michael was the Kings' second child and first son. In 1931, Michael King, Sr., began calling himself Martin Luther King. He began calling his son Martin Luther King, Jr.

Martin Luther King, Jr. studied at Morehouse College in Atlanta, Georgia. During his last semester, King was ordained as a minister. After leaving Morehouse, King entered the Crozer Theological Seminary in Pennsylvania to study religion more deeply. In 1951, King began studying religion at Boston University.

But, in 1954, King accepted a job as the minister at Dexter Avenue Baptist Church in Montgomery, Alabama. In December 1966, King was elected to head a new group called the Montgomery Improvement Association. The group protested the arrest of Rosa Parks for refusing to give up her seat on the bus to a white man.

King used religion and peace to share his feelings about racism in the United States. He was a leader in the movement to give African Americans the same rights as white Americans. Using peaceful means, King was able to convince people to help make the United States a more equal nation.

On April 4, 1968, King's years of nonviolent leadership were cut short by an assassin's bullet. Leaders of all races and political beliefs attended King's funeral in his hometown of Atlanta.

- 1944–1948 attended Morehouse College in Atlanta
- 1948–1951 attended Crozer Theological Seminary in PA
- 1951–1955 attended Boston University's School of Theology
- 1953 married Coretta Scott
- 1955 asked to serve as leader for the Montgomery Bus Boycott
- 1957 elected president of Southern Baptist Leadership Conference
- 1963 led coalition of civil rights group in nonviolent demonstration aimed at Birmingham, AL
- 1963 March on Washington and famous "I Have a Dream" speech
- 1964 became youngest person to win Nobel Peace Prize
- 1964 Congress passed Civil Rights Act
- 1965 Congress passed Voting Rights Act
- 1968 King assassinated

| 1945 | 1950 | 1955 | 1960 | 1965 | 1970 |

MARTIN LUTHER KING, JR.

Martin Luther King, Jr. was an inspiring man. He was probably one of the greatest men who have ever lived. His life was an example of simple living and great thinking. One of King's greatest quotes was, "Now is the time to lift our national policy from the quicksand of racial injustice to the solid rock of human dignity." These words speak to King's dedication to human rights in the United States. Read the timeline below to learn more about this amazing man.

- 1929 Martin Luther King, Jr. was born in Atlanta, Georgia. His name at birth was Michael Luther King, but he later changed it to Martin.
- 1944 At the age of 15, he graduated from high school.
- 1953 Martin Luther King, Jr. married Coretta Scott.
- 1955 He earned a doctorate degree in philosophy from Boston University; he became the president of the Montgomery Improvement Association (MIA).
- 1957 Martin Luther King, Jr. spoke to a gathering of more than 15,000 people in Washington D.C.
- 1959 He visited India, the land of Gandhi.
- 1962 Martin Luther King, Jr. participated in many Civil Rights movements and was sent to jail many times.
- 1963 He attended many Civil Rights movements; he was sent to jail in Birmingham.
- 1968 Martin Luther King, Jr. was shot to death while at the Lorraine Motel.

| 1930 | 1940 | 1950 | 1960 | 1970 |

English Language Arts

Compare Two Texts
Reading: Informational Text

Strategy — Look carefully at visuals to see how they connect to the information in the passage.

Test Tip — Compare the information in the two timelines. Sometimes, timelines of the same person or event include different information.

1. What is the main idea of both passages?

(A) Martin Luther King, Jr. was born in Atlanta, Georgia.

(B) When Martin Luther King, Jr. was named Michael.

(C) Martin Luther King, Jr. was a great part of American history.

(D) Martin Luther King, Jr. was assassinated in 1968.

Write how you know.

_____

_____

_____

_____

2. Write three details from the passages that support the main idea.

_____

_____

_____

_____

_____

_____

_____

_____

3. How are the two passages different?

_____

_____

_____

_____

4. How are the two timelines different?

_____

_____

_____

_____

_____

_____

5. Explain how reading both passages helps you understand the topic.

_____

_____

_____

_____

_____

English Language Arts

Determine the Meaning of Words and Phrases
Language

DIRECTIONS: Read the passage. Then, answer the questions.

How much do you know about snakes? Read these snake facts and find out.
- A snake skeleton has numerous ribs. A large snake may have as many as 400 pairs!
- Most snakes have poor eyesight. They track other animals by sensing their body heat.
- Snakes can't blink! They sleep with their eyes open.
- Although snakes have teeth, only the venomous ones have fangs.
- Many snakes are docile and unlikely to bite people.
- Pet snakes recognize their owners by smell. They flick their tongues in the air to detect smells.
- Snakes have special ways of hearing. Sound vibrations in the ground pass through their bellies to receptors in their spines. Airborne sounds pass through snakes' lungs to receptors in their skin.

Strategy Clarify word meanings by using key words.

Test Tip If you are unsure of an answer, try to eliminate answers you know are not correct. Then, reread parts of the passage to determine the correct answer.

1. In this passage, *poor* means the opposite of _____.
   - (A) rich
   - (B) good
   - (C) happy
   - (D) broke

2. What does *track* mean, as it is used in this passage?

_____

_____

Write how you know.

_____

_____

_____

_____

3. What does the word *venomous* mean, as it is used in this passage?

_____

What is the root word of venomous?

_____

4. Rewrite this sentence using the antonym of docile:

"Many snakes are docile and unlikely to bite people."

_____

_____

English Language Arts

Determine the Meaning of Words and Phrases
Language

DIRECTIONS: Read the passage. Then, answer the questions.

> Ancient myths often depict monsters with multiple heads. But, that may not be so far from reality. A 2-headed snake is rare, but they do exist.
>
> A 2-headed snake was discovered in Spain. This snake is not poisonous. It was a 2-month-old ladder snake that was about 8 inches long. The snake was lucky to be captured, since it would not have had much chance of surviving in the wild.
>
> The snake takes a long time to eat, making it vulnerable to predators. While feeding, the 2 heads fight over which will swallow the food. Additionally, because snakes use their sense of smell to find food, if one head smells prey on the other head, it will attack it.
>
> The heads also have a hard time deciding which direction to go. If it were attacked, it would have a hard time escaping.
>
> Two-headed snakes do not seem to be a product of evolution. Much like conjoined twins, it appears that the embryo, or egg, starts to split into 2 but does not complete the division.
>
> Although 2-headed snakes can survive in captivity, their chances of surviving in the wild are almost zero.

Strategy   Determine the meaning of unknown words by identifying synonyms and antonyms.

Test Tip   Make sure you read all of the answer choices. When you think you see the correct answer, place your finger next to it.

1. Which word is a synonym for *vulnerable*?

(A) safe

(B) helpless

(C) dangerous

(D) scary

Write how you know.

_____

_____

_____

_____

2. What is prey?

_____

_____

3. What do you think *conjoined* means?

(A) separate

(B) identical

(C) fraternal

(D) attached

Which words in the passage helped you choose the meaning?

_____

_____

4. What is an *embryo*?

_____

English Language Arts

Write an Informative/Explanatory Text
Writing

DIRECTIONS: Read the paragraph below about how to plant a seed. Then, think of something you know how to do well. Write a procedure that explains how to do it. Use paragraphs and words such as *first, next, then, finally,* and *last.*

Strategy   When you write to inform or explain, gather the facts you will present about a topic. Think about experiences you have had and information you already know.

I learned how to plant a seed and make it grow. First, I found a spot where the plant would get the right amount of sunshine. Next, I dug a hole, put the seed into the soil, and covered the seed with soil. Then, I watered the seed. After a couple weeks, it began to grow into a beautiful plant.

_____

_____

_____

_____

_____

_____

_____

_____

_____

_____

_____

_____

_____

_____

_____

_____

_____

Name _____ Date _____

Write an Informative/Explanatory Text
Writing

DIRECTIONS: Ethan was working on a report for his class. He could write about any animal he chose. Ethan loved owls and decided to make them the topic of his report. Before he started writing, he developed the following outline. Study the outline, and then answer the questions that follow.

Strategy — Use graphic organizers to help you put facts and ideas in the right order.

Test Tip — If information is not given in an order that makes sense, readers won't understand the passage.

OWLS

I. _____
   A. Great Horned Owl
   B. Snowy Owl
   C. Barn Owl
II. **Body Characteristics**
   A. Size
   B. Body Covering
   C. _____
   D. Eyes, Talons, and Beaks
III. **Eating Habits**
   A. Mice
   B. Other Small Rodents

1. Which best fits the blank next to I?

Ⓐ Owl Migration

Ⓑ Owl Habitats

Ⓒ Types of Owls

Ⓓ Owl Eating Habits

2. Which best fits the blank next to C?

Ⓐ Feather Variations

Ⓑ Grasses and Leaves

Ⓒ Trees

Ⓓ Nocturnal

3. Explain how the organization of the outline will help Ethan write his report.

_____

_____

_____

_____

_____

_____

_____

_____

English Language Arts

Write an Informative/Explanatory Text
Writing

DIRECTIONS: An informative passage gives facts and details about a topic. Write an informative passage about an animal you know about well. Your report should have the following:

- A sentence to introduce your topic
- Facts about your topic
- Definitions and details about your topic
- Categories of information
- SpecIfic words to explain the topic
- A sentence to end your paragraph

Strategy   Plan your writing. Use an outline like the one Ethan made to make your writing clear and organized.

Test Tip   Try to think of at least two details for each piece of information in your plan.

Topic: _____

   I. _____

      A. _____

      B. _____

      C. _____

  II. _____

      A. _____

      B. _____

      C. _____

      D. _____

 III. _____

      A. _____

      B. _____

English Language Arts

Write an Informative/Explanatory Text
Writing

DIRECTIONS: Write your paragraph on the lines. Use the checklist to make sure your paragraph is organized clearly and includes all of the information.

Test Tip   Use your outline as you write your informational passage to present your ideas and facts clearly.

Checklist

☐ I introduced my topic.

☐ I gave at least three facts about my topic.

☐ I supported my facts with details.

☐ I grouped information together.

☐ I used specific words.

☐ I have a good conclusion.

_____

_____

_____

_____

_____

_____

_____

_____

_____

_____

_____

_____

_____

_____

English Language Arts

Write a Narrative
Writing

DIRECTIONS: A narrative is a story that tells about real or imagined events. Write a narrative about a problem you had and how you solved it. Your paragraph should have the following:

- A narrator and/or characters
- A natural sequence of events
- Dialogue
- Descriptions of actions, thoughts, and feelings
- Time words and phrases to show the order of events
- Concrete words and sensory details
- A sentence to end your paragraph

Strategy Plan a narrative by choosing people, places, and events that will be in the story. Remember that a story should have a beginning, middle, and end.

Test Tip Include details that help your readers understand the event and imagine it in their minds.

Situation or Problem:
Event 1:
Details:
Event 2:
Details:
Event 3:
Details:
Conclusion:

Write a Narrative
Writing

DIRECTIONS: Write your paragraph on the lines. Use the checklist to make sure your paragraph is organized clearly and includes all of the information.

Test Tip   Use your organizer as you write your narrative to make sure events are in order and that you use details.

Checklist

☐ I introduced my narrator and/or characters.

☐ I told what the problem in the story was.

☐ I wrote a clear sequence of events that happened.

☐ I used dialogue and wrote about the characters' thoughts, actions, and feelings.

☐ I used time words.

☐ I used concrete words and sensory details.

☐ I have a good conclusion.

_____

_____

_____

_____

_____

_____

_____

_____

_____

_____

_____

_____

_____

_____

English Language Arts

Understand Editing and Revising
Writing

DIRECTIONS: Choose or write the best answer.

> **Strategy**
> Revise to make sure your writing makes sense. Then, edit to fix errors. Use what you know about nouns, verbs, adjectives, and adverbs to make correct choices when you edit.

> **Test Tip**
> When you are revising a paragraph, read it out loud to yourself. Listen for anything that does not sound right or does not make sense.

1. Rewrite the following fragments as complete sentences.

playing outside

_____

a few people in this class

_____

on the roof

_____

in the air

_____

2. Explain why it is important to use complete sentences in writing.

_____

_____

_____

3. Find the word that is spelled correctly and that best fits the sentence.

Please _____ your work before turning it in.

- (A) revew
- (B) reeview
- (C) review
- (D) reveiw

He is my best _____.

- (A) frind
- (B) frend
- (C) friend
- (D) freind

We _____ her to arrive at noon.

- (A) acept
- (B) espect
- (C) accept
- (D) expect

4. Rewrite the sentences using correct capitalization and punctuation.

tyson began singing the star-spangled banner

_____

_____

I'm really glad you are here abby said

_____

_____

5. Combine the two simple sentences into a compound sentence.

Sasha flew to Chicago. She took a train to Milwaukee.

_____

English Language Arts

Understand Editing and Revising
Writing

DIRECTIONS: Choose or write the best answer.

> **Strategy**
> Reread your writing out loud to find punctuation mistakes. To find spelling and capitalization errors, try reading backward, looking at each word.

1. Use each word or phrase in a sentence.

whom

_____

_____

where

_____

_____

will be going

_____

_____

must

_____

_____

2. Which sentences are written correctly? Choose all that apply.

   (A) We went to there house.

   (B) I gave them their gifts.

   (C) Two of the birds flew away.

   (D) I was to late to see the movie.

3. Revise the story so it sounds better. Choose words and phrases that precisely show ideas and punctuation for effect.

I saw this thing on the street. It was a red, big bag. I wondered what was in it. I looked inside. It was something round and small. It was something shiny. I had found a gold coin.

_____

_____

_____

_____

_____

_____

_____

_____

_____

_____

_____

_____

English Language Arts

Strategy Review

In this section, you will review the strategies you learned and apply them to practice the skills.

Strategy | Use details from the story to make inferences, understand theme, and determine meaning.

EXAMPLE

Read the story carefully. Then, answer the questions using details from the story.

A BUMPY RIDE

When we first climbed into the car and strapped on our safety belts, I wasn't very nervous. I was sitting right next to my big brother, and he had done this many times before. As we started to climb the hill, however, I could feel my heart jump into my throat.

"Brian?" I asked nervously. "Is this supposed to be so noisy?"

"Sure, Matthew," Brian answered. "It always does that."

A minute later, we were going so fast down the hill, I didn't have time to think. With a twist, a loop, and a bunch of fast turns, everyone on board screamed in delight. No wonder this was one of the most popular rides in the park. By the time the car pulled into the station and we got off the ride, I was ready to do it again!

How does the description of the scene help you know the setting of the story?

The story describes a car with a safety belt climbing a hill and then going fast down a hill, around turns, and through twists and loops. This tells you that the setting is an amusement park and the boys are on a roller coaster.

1. How did the character's feelings change throughout the story?

_____

_____

_____

_____

_____

2. How do you think Matthew will feel the next time he gets on a roller coaster?

_____

3. How did the strategy help you answer these questions?

_____

_____

_____

_____

_____

_____

Strategy Review

DIRECTIONS: Read the story carefully. Then, answer the questions.

Strategy Look carefully at visuals such as illustrations, diagrams, or graphs to see how they connect to the story.

Most Popular Sports at Lake Bluff Elementary School

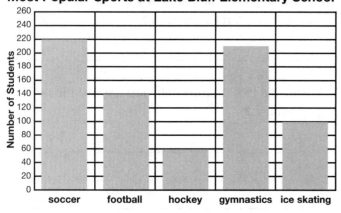

Describe what this graph is about.

To understand a visual within a passage, look at the words around and on the visual. This is a bar graph. Notice sports along the bottom and numbers along the side. The title tells you this graph is about popular sports at an elementary school.

1. **What is the most popular sport at Lake Bluff Elementary School?**

   (A) soccer

   (B) football

   (C) gymnastics

   (D) ice skating

2. **In what type of passage would you expect to see a graph like this?**

   _____

   _____

THE UN-BIRTHDAY

In my family, we don't celebrate birthdays—at least not like most families. My friends say I have an "un-birthday." The tradition started with my grandmother. She and my grandfather grew up in Poland. They escaped before World War II and made their way to America. When they arrived, they were so grateful, they decided to share what they had with others. On their birthdays, they gave each other just one small gift. Then, they each bought a gift for someone who needed it more than they did.

As you read, think about how the story compares to what you know and how you celebrate birthdays in your family.

3. **How would you describe an un-birthday to someone?**

   _____

   _____

   _____

   _____

4. **Why did the narrator's grandparents decide to celebrate an un-birthday?**

   _____

   _____

   _____

   _____

Strategy

Reread stories to make comparisons, draw conclusions, or support inferences.

Strategy Review

> **Strategy** | Identify a story's structure, see how ideas are related, and clarify word meanings by using word clues.

Ethan and Austin have two dogs. Both dogs are about the same age. Sam is 6 years old, and Xavier is 7 years old.

Sam is a Collie-Shepherd mix. He is black with a white chest. Sam weighs 75 pounds. In the winter, Sam's fur grows very long. He looks like a shaggy black bear. Sam has a straight tail with lots of fur hanging off of it.

Xavier is a Chow-Labrador mix. He is tan. His fur is very short, and his tail curls up toward his back. Xavier also weighs about 75 pounds.

Both dogs are very sweet. They let the boys use them as pillows. They like to run and play in the backyard. Sam likes to chase balls and bring them back to be thrown again. But, Xavier just likes to eat them.

When you read the story, words like *both* and *also* tell you the dogs are being compared. Words like *but* tell you the dogs are being contrasted.

1. How are Sam and Xavier alike?

_____

_____

_____

2. How are Sam and Xavier different?

_____

_____

_____

> **Strategy**
>
> Use an outline to plan your writing.

Before you start writing, make a plan of what you are going to include. Use an outline or other graphic organizer to keep your ideas in order.

EXAMPLE

Write a report about horses.

I. Breeds
  A. Abaco Barb
  B. American Paint Horse
  C. Andalusia

II. Appearances
  A. Hair
  B. Mane
  C. Tail

III. Interesting Facts
  A. Where are they from?
  B. How are they used?
  C. Horse History

3. Use an outline to plan a report about an animal.

I. _____

  A. _____

  B. _____

  C. _____

II. _____

  A. _____

  B. _____

  C. _____

III. _____

  A. _____

  B. _____

  C. _____

Strategy Review

Strategy | When writing, use details to support, explain, or clarify your main ideas. Use the plan you made to guide your writing.

EXAMPLE

This is an example of a report about horses.

There are many different breeds, or kinds, of horses. Some horse breeds are the Abaco Barb, the American Paint Horse, and the Andalusia.

The Abaco Barb has bay-, brown-, or pinto-colored hair. Its mane and tail are thick and long. The tail is set low on its body. The American Paint Horse is white combined with different-colored markings. These markings can be any other color in which you might find a horse and vary in size and location. Most Andalusia horses are gray, but other colors can be found.

The Abaco Barb is in danger of becoming extinct. There are only 8 of these horses left. They live on an island in the Bahamas. These horses are descended from Spanish horses believed to have been on ships to the New World during the time of Christopher Columbus.

Now, use your outline you wrote to write a paragraph about a specific animal.

_____

_____

_____

_____

_____

_____

_____

_____

_____

_____

Strategy

Revise to make sure your writing is clear and makes sense. Then, edit to fix errors.

Look for words that need capital letters.

Look for places that need punctuation.

Read the sentences carefully to see if they make sense.

Rewrite the sentences on the lines so that they are clear and correct.

1. sheri said I would really like some ice cream

_____

_____

_____

2. Do yoy think they will want us to go to great america with them

_____

_____

_____

3. How many times have you seen the movie when you were little

_____

_____

_____

Strategies for Mathematics Tests

Read the strategies below to learn more about how they work.

Use rules, properties, or formulas to solve problems.

You can use rules, properties, and formulas to solve a variety of problems. For example, if you know the formula for the area of a rectangle, you can use a given length and width of the rectangle (or a rectangular garden) to quickly find its area. If you understand the commutative and distributive properties, you can rearrange an equation to solve it. If you understand the rules of the order of operations, you can correctly evaluate a mathematical expression.

Use drawings, graphs, or number lines to understand and solve a problem.

Many problems on a test can be modeled with a quick sketch, graph, or number line. These drawings can help you visualize the problem, figure out what you are being asked to find, or solve word problems.

Read word problems carefully to identify the given information and what you are being asked to find.

Whenever you encounter a word problem, you should first ask *What is the given information?* Then, you should ask *What question am I being asked to answer?* or *What am I being asked to find?* Don't start your calculations until you know the answers to these questions!

Look for key words in word problems that help you know which operation to use.

Key words in problems are signals that you should use certain operations. For example, the words *how much less* indicate subtraction. The words *total* and *altogether* often indicate addition. If you are asked to split something into equal portions, use division.

Organize and display data in order to interpret it.

Interpreting data means finding meaning in it. One way to find meaning in data is to organize it in a visual way. For example, dot plots are great for understanding data from a survey or poll. Line graphs show how two sets of data are related.

Apply prior knowledge and basic operations to solve problems.

Using what you already know about numbers and about the basic operations addition, subtraction, multiplication, and division, you can solve problems involving decimals, fractions, geometry, and converting units of measurement. For example, you can use your understanding of division, multiplication, and place value to find area and to convert meters to centimeters.

Write and solve equations to solve real-world problems.

Translating everyday language into equations that use numbers, variables, and operations signs is an essential strategy. You will need to combine your understanding of several strategies to write and solve these equations, including understanding basic operations; applying rules, properties, and formulas; and looking for clues in the words to find needed information.

Interpret a Multiplication Equation as a Comparison

Operations and Algebraic Thinking

DIRECTIONS: Choose or write the correct answer.

Strategy   Use multiplication to solve comparison problems.

EXAMPLE

Sari is 8 years old. Her grandmother is 7 times as old as Sari. Write an equation to show how old Sari's grandmother is.

Answer: $8 \times 7 = 56$

Sari's grandmother is 56 years old.

1. Charlie uses plastic blocks to make a 12-story building. He uses 48 blocks for the first 3 floors of the building. He uses 10 times as many blocks to complete all 12 floors. Which equation can be used to find how many blocks Charlie uses to make the 12-story building?

   Ⓐ $48 \times 3 = 144$

   Ⓑ $48 \times 10 = 480$

   Ⓒ $12 \times 10 = 120$

   Ⓓ $48 \times 12 = 576$

Test Tip

A *multiplicative comparison* is when one quantity is multiplied by a specified number to find another quantity.

2. Jeremy has 7 books about robots. Carlo has 4 times the number of robot books that Jeremy has. Which equation represents the number of robot books Carlo has?

   Ⓐ $4 \times 11 = 44$

   Ⓑ $4 + 7 = 11$

   Ⓒ $4 \times 8 = 32$

   Ⓓ $4 \times 7 = 28$

3. A package of red pencils has 8 pencils. A package of black pencils has 5 times as many pencils. How many total pencils are in the package of black pencils?

_____

4. Write an equation that means 42 is 6 times as many as 7.

5. What is another correct representation of the equation in Question 4?

   Ⓐ 6 is 42 times as many as 7

   Ⓑ 7 is 6 times as many as 42

   Ⓒ 42 is 7 times as many as 6

   Ⓓ 7 is 42 times as many as 6

6. Arnie and Jason are playing a card game. Arnie has 9 points. Jason has 4 times as many points as Arnie has. Jason writes this number sentence to help him find how many more points he has than Arnie. Finish the equation. Then, find how many more points Jason has than Arnie.

$$\boxed{} = 9 \times 4$$

Solve Multiplicative Comparison Problems: Multiply and Divide

Operations and Algebraic Thinking

DIRECTIONS: Choose or write the correct answer.

> ## Strategy
> Use multiplication and division to solve multiplicative comparison problems.

EXAMPLE

A music CD costs $9 on sale. A movie DVD on sale costs 3 times as much. How much does the movie DVD cost?

Write an equation and solve it. Let *c* represent the cost of the DVD.

$c = 9 \times 3$

$c = 27$

The movie DVD costs $27.

> ## Test Tip
> This is one kind of *multiplicative comparison* problem where you are finding an unknown product.

1. Andrea built a small puzzle with 72 pieces. This is 3 times as many pieces as in Kyle's puzzle. Which equation can be used to find how many pieces, *p*, are in Kyle's puzzle?

   (A) $72 \div 3 = p$

   (B) $72 \times 3 = p$

   (C) $72 + 3 = p$

   (D) $72 - 3 = p$

2. A flea can jump 130 times its own height. If you could do the same, and your height is 54 inches, which equation could you solve to find how high, *h*, you could jump?

   (A) $h = 130 + 54$

   (B) $h = 130 \times 54$

   (C) $54 = h \times 130$

   (D) $130 = 54 \times h$

3. There are 9 boys in the cafeteria line. There are 2 times as many girls in the cafeteria line. Write a number sentence that can be used to find *g*, the number of girls in the line. Then, solve the number sentence.

_____

4. A cook is making pasta sauce. She has 64 tomatoes. She also has green peppers. The number of tomatoes is 8 times the number of peppers. Write a division equation and multiplication equation that can be used to find the number of peppers, *p*, the cook has. Solve the equation.

Solve Multiplicative Comparison Problems: Multiply and Divide
Operations and Algebraic Thinking

DIRECTIONS: Choose or write the correct answer.

5. **Rianna has 24 stickers. This is 4 times the number of stickers that Alonzo has. Which of these show how to find how many stickers, s, Alonzo has? Choose all that apply.**

Ⓐ 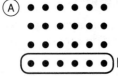 Number of stickers Alonzo has

Ⓑ $4 \times s = 24$

Ⓒ 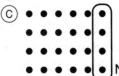 Number of stickers Alonzo has

Ⓓ $24 + 24 + 24 + 24 = s$

Test Tip

Making a drawing can help you visualize a problem.

6. **Michiko loves flowers. She has 4 huge sunflowers in her garden and 5 times as many red rose bushes as sunflowers. She has 2 times as many yellow rose bushes as red ones. How many yellow rose bushes are in Michiko's garden? Show your work.**

7. **Diane's grandfather is 63 years old. The equation shows he is 7 times as old as Diane. How many years old is Diane? Show how you know.**

$$63 = 7 \times \square$$

_____

_____

_____

_____

8. **Sylvia and Marta are each making a paper link chain to decorate for the class party. Sylvia's chain is 28 inches long. This is 4 times the length of Marta's chain, m. Which equation can be used to find out how long Marta's chain is? Choose all that apply.**

Ⓐ $28 \times 4 = m$

Ⓑ $m \times 28 = 4$

Ⓒ $28 \div 4 = m$

Ⓓ $m \times 4 = 28$

Solve Multi-Step Problems: Add, Subtract, Multiply, and Divide

Operations and Algebraic Thinking

DIRECTIONS: Choose or write the correct answer.

Strategy   Use the order of operations as you solve problems.

EXAMPLE

Sarah, Dora, and Ruby had $45 to spend at the mall. They spent $15 on food and evenly split the rest. How much did each girl get? Show how you got your answer.

This is a multi-step problem. Write an equation and solve it. Let m represent how much money each girl gets.

$m = (45 - 15) \div 3$

$m = 30 \div 3$

$m = 10$

Each girl gets $10.

1. Simon is helping his younger brother build a tower with 88 blocks. For the bottom layer, Simon makes 5 rows with 4 blocks in each row. How many blocks are left to build the rest of the tower?

    (A) 81 blocks

    (B) 79 blocks

    (C) 83 blocks

    (D) 68 blocks

2. For three days, Jon and his friends collected toys for their school's annual toy drive. Their work is shown in the table below. They will give the same number of toys to 4 different childcare centers. Write and solve an equation to find the number of toys, n, that each center will get.

Day	Number of Toys
Monday	36
Tuesday	67
Wednesday	53

3. Mr. Gomez owns a sports store. He orders 24 caps from Company A and 35 caps from Company B. When they arrive, he places them on shelves that hold 9 caps each. How many shelves will Mr. Gomez need to hold all the caps? Show your work.

Test Tip

Remember the order of operations when you solve multi-step problems. Do operations inside parentheses first, and multiply and divide before you add and subtract.

4. Sari and her family drove $9\frac{1}{2}$ hours to the beach. On the first day, they drove 289 miles. On the second day, they drove 377 miles. If they drove at a steady rate each day with no stops, which is the best estimate of how many miles per hour they drove?

    (A) 70 miles per hour

    (B) 50 miles per hour

    (C) 60 miles per hour

    (D) 74 miles per hour

5. Explain how you got your answer in Question 4.

_____

_____

Solve Multi-Step Problems: Add, Subtract, Multiply, and Divide
Operations and Algebraic Thinking

DIRECTIONS: Choose or write the correct answer.

> **Strategy** — Use basic operations rules. For multi-step problems, complete operations from left to right.

6. Clarissa was paid $216 for 3 days of work. She worked 8 hours each day. Which can you use to find how much Clarissa earned per hour? Choose all that apply.

   Ⓐ $216 \times 3 \div 8$

   Ⓑ $8 \times 3 \div 216$

   Ⓒ $216 \div 3 \div 8$

   Ⓓ $216 \div 8 \div 3$

> **Test Tip**
>
> Multiply and divide left to right, and then, add and subtract left to right.

DIRECTIONS: Use the information below to answer Questions 7 and 8.

> Jamie read for 30 minutes on Monday, 47 minutes on Tuesday, 64 minutes on Wednesday, and 81 minutes on Thursday. On Friday, Jamie spent 15 fewer minutes reading than on Monday.

7. How many total minutes did Jamie spend reading those days? Show your work.

8. How many hours and minutes is this? Show how you know.

9. Three friends are counting their sports cards and putting them in plastic bags to trade. Oliver has 72 cards and Casey has 56 cards. If they put them in bags of 8 cards each, how many bags will they need? Show two ways you can solve this problem.

10. In the school band, 3 rows of students play trumpet, 2 rows play trombone, and 1 row plays drums. If there are 10 students in each row, how many students are in the band?

   Ⓐ 50 students

   Ⓑ 60 students

   Ⓒ 30 students

   Ⓓ 16 students

Find Factors and Multiples
Operations and Algebraic Thinking

DIRECTIONS: Choose or write the correct answer.

Strategy   Use factors and multiples to find the answer.

EXAMPLE

Factors are numbers multiplied together to obtain a product. A *multiple* is the product of a given whole number and any other whole number.

Factors of 36: 1, 2, 3, 4, 6, 9, 12

Some multiples of 6: 30, 36, 42, 48

1. Which shows all of the factors of 15?

Ⓐ 1, 15

Ⓑ 1, 3, 15

Ⓒ 1, 3, 5, 15

Ⓓ 5, 10, 15, 20

2. All even numbers are multiples of what number?

Ⓐ 1

Ⓑ 2

Ⓒ 4

Ⓓ 10

3. List all of the factor pairs of 56.

_____

_____

Test Tip

A prime number is a number greater than 1 that has only 2 factors: 1 and itself. Composite numbers have more than 2 factors.

4. Ginny's brother's age is a prime number between 12 and 20. Which number could be his age? Choose all that apply.

Ⓐ 15

Ⓑ 13

Ⓒ 19

Ⓓ 17

5. DIRECTIONS: Use the numbers in the box to complete the table below. Some numbers may not be used. Some numbers may be used more than once.

4 8 12 16 18 48 68 96 144

Multiples of 48	Factors of 48

6. Which are the prime number factors of 12?

Ⓐ 2, 3, 4

Ⓑ 24, 36, 48

Ⓒ 2, 6

Ⓓ 1, 2, 3

7. Lucinda has 78 books on her shelves. Is 78 a prime or a composite number? Write how you know.

_____

_____

_____

_____

Analyze Patterns
Operations and Algebraic Thinking

DIRECTIONS: Choose or write the correct answer.

Strategy — Find features in the pattern to determine what comes next and to identify the rule.

EXAMPLE

What is the rule? Find the pattern in the row of numbers. Fill in the blanks with the missing numbers to complete the pattern.

64, 54, 44, ___, ___, 14, ___

Rule: Subtract 10.

Missing numbers: 34, 24, 4

1. **Look at the pattern. Which shape comes next?**

(A)

(B)

(C)

(D)

2. **DIRECTIONS:** Look for a pattern in the IN and OUT numbers in the table. Fill in the table. Then, write the rule.

IN	2	9	81	76	37		
OUT	11	18		85		34	51

Rule: _____

_____

_____

DIRECTIONS: For Questions 3 and 4, write the missing numbers. Then, write the rule.

3. **88, ____, 66, ____, 44, ____, ____**

Missing numbers: _____

Rule: _____

4. **17, 25, 33, ____, ____, ____**

Missing numbers: _____

Rule: _____

5. **Which number pattern follows the rule "multiply by 6"?**

(A) 6, 12, 24, 48

(B) 1, 7, 13, 19

(C) 6, 6, 12, 12

(D) 1, 6, 36, 216

6. **Start with the number 78. Write the missing numbers using the rule "add 4."**

78, _____, _____, _____, _____, _____, _____

Round Numbers to 1,000,000
Numbers and Operations in Base Ten

DIRECTIONS: Choose or write the correct answer.

> ## Strategy   Use rounding to estimate numbers and answer the questions.

EXAMPLE

Round 146,472 to the nearest ten, hundred, thousand, and ten thousand.

Nearest ten: 146,470

Nearest thousand: 146,000

Nearest hundred: 146,500

Nearest ten thousand: 150,000

Test Tip

When rounding numbers, look to the next numeral of lesser value. If the numeral is 5, 6, 7, 8, or 9, round the previous numeral up. If the numeral is 0, 1, 2, 3, or 4, round the previous numeral down.

1. The number of people watching a hockey game is 900 when rounded to the nearest hundred and 850 when rounded to the nearest ten. Which of these could be the number of people watching the game?

- (A) 847
- (B) 849
- (C) 856
- (D) 852

2. Which of these numbers shows 587 rounded to the nearest hundred?

- (A) 580
- (B) 600
- (C) 690
- (D) 500

3. Which would you use to estimate 97 + 9 to the nearest 10?

- (A) 90 + 5
- (B) 100 + 10
- (C) 90 + 10
- (D) 100 + 5

4. Write two numbers that round to 35,000 when rounded to the nearest thousand. The first number should be less than 35,000, and the second number should be greater than 35,000.

_____

_____

_____

5. The population of Wyoming is 577,412. What is this number rounded to the nearest ten thousand? Write how you know.

_____

_____

_____

_____

_____

6. The diameter of Earth is 7,926 miles. The diameter of Jupiter is 88,846 miles. Round each number to the nearest thousand.

_____

_____

_____

Add and Subtract Multi-Digit Whole Numbers
Numbers and Operations in Base Ten

DIRECTIONS: Choose or write the correct answer.

> ### Strategy
> Find words that are clues to the operation to use by reading word problems carefully.

EXAMPLE

The school band has two shows every year. A total of 458 people went to the shows. If 305 people went to the first show, how many people went to the second show?

First, decide what operation you will use to solve the problem: subtraction

Next, subtract: 458 − 305 = 153

153 people went to the second show.

1. There were 258 cans of soup on the grocery store shelf in the morning. At 1:00 p.m., there were 156 cans of soup on the shelf. By the time the store closed at 7:00 p.m., 100 more cans of soup had been sold. How many cans of soup did the store sell the entire day?

   (A) 202 cans

   (B) 102 cans

   (C) 56 cans

   (D) 256 cans

2. How did you get your answer in Question 2?

3. A desk normally costs $129. It is on sale for $99. How much would you save if you bought 2 desks on sale?

   (A) $114

   (B) $15

   (C) $60

   (D) $198

4. The highway department uses 6 gallons of paint for every 10 blocks of highway stripe. Write an equation and solve it to find how many gallons will be needed for 250 blocks of highway stripe.

5. The base of Summit Mountain is 5,456 feet above sea level. The top of the mountain is 10,700 feet above sea level. How many feet is it from the base to the top of the mountain? Show your work.

6. Anna flew from New York to Paris, France, a distance of 3,627 miles. Then, she flew from Paris to Beijing, China, a distance of 5,106 miles. How many total miles did Anna fly?

> ### Test Tip
> When adding or subtracting, be sure you align the numbers so the place values match.

Multiply Whole Numbers Using Strategies
Numbers and Operations in Base Ten

DIRECTIONS: Choose or write the correct answer.

Strategy | Use or sketch models, drawings, or numbers when multiplying.

EXAMPLE

Twenty-seven students each brought 1 dozen cookies to the class bake sale. How many cookies did they bring?

12 × 27 = c

Using a place value strategy, you can reduce 12 to 10 and 2.

227 × 10 = 270

27 × 2 = 54

270 + 54 = 324

They brought 324 cookies.

DIRECTIONS: Use the information below to answer Questions 1 and 2.

Nolan gathered eggs from his chickens. He filled 43 cartons, with 12 eggs in each carton. To find the total number of eggs, Nolan first multiplied 10 by 43 and then multiplied 2 by 43.

1. What is the next step to find the total number of eggs?

2. How many eggs did Nolan gather?

_____

3. Sophie joined a baseball league that has 38 players. Their uniforms cost $40 each. What is the total cost of the players' uniforms? Use your understanding of place value to explain how you found your answer.

4. The running club is planning a bus trip to the next race. There are 64 members in the club. Each member has to pay $10 for the bus ride. How much money will the trip cost?

5. Explain what happens to a value when it is multiplied by 10. Use the numbers in Question 4 in your explanation.

6. Serena solved the problem 35 × 26 this way. Show why the answer is not correct. Include the correct answer.

$$\begin{array}{r} 26 \\ \times\ 35 \\ \hline 130 \\ +\ 78 \\ \hline 208 \end{array}$$

Multiply Whole Numbers Using Strategies
Numbers and Operations in Base Ten

DIRECTIONS: Choose or write the correct answer.

> **Strategy**   Multiply whole numbers using strategies based on place value and properties of operations.

7. **Clarissa earns $56 every week walking her neighbor's two dogs. How much money does she earn in one year?**

   (A) $2,602

   (B) $2,800

   (C) $2,912

   (D) $2,612

8. **Griffin is selling popcorn for the school fundraiser. He sells 13 original boxes for $7 each and 15 super boxes for $12 each. How much money did he earn for the fundraiser? Write and solve an equation.**

9. **Hector said the product of 4,673 and 4 is 18,412. Here is his work. Find Hector's error. Then, write the correct product.**

   $$(4{,}000 \times 4) + (600 \times 4) + (3 \times 4)$$

10. **20 × 25 is the same as _____**

    (A) 20 × 5 × 5

    (B) 20 × 20 × 5

    (C) 10 × 10 × 25

    (D) 20 × 4 × 5

> **Test Tip**
>
> Remember, to find the area, multiply length by width.

11. **Bethany is helping her grandpa put new tile on the kitchen floor. The floor surface measures 14 feet wide by 18 feet long. Each tile can cover an area of 2 square feet. How many tiles, *t*, will they need to cover the floor surface? Write and solve an equation.**

Divide Whole Numbers Using Strategies
Numbers and Operations in Base Ten

DIRECTIONS: Choose or write the correct answer.

Strategy Divide whole numbers using strategies based on place value and properties of operations.

EXAMPLE

Mr. Larson has a vegetable garden. There are a total of 294 vegetable plants in 7 rows, with an equal number of plants in each row. How many plants are in each of the 7 rows in Mr. Larson's garden?

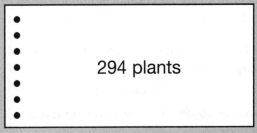

Divide to find the answer. 294 ÷ 7 = 42
There are 42 plants in each row.

1. Ken works 8 hours a day at the widget factory. He assembles the same number of widgets every hour. If he assembles 1,752 widgets a day, how many widgets does he assemble per hour?

   (A) 200
   (B) 219
   (C) 209
   (D) 305

2. Jacob has a bag with 124 game tokens. His father puts 68 more tokens into the bag. Jacob now shares the tokens with 3 friends. How many tokens, *t*, do Jacob and his friends each receive? Write an equation. Then, solve it.

   _____

   _____

3. There are 3 sports stadiums in the city where Tomas lives. One weekend, a total of 6,693 people watched events at the 3 stadiums. The same number of people were at each stadium. Which equation can be used to find how many people were at each stadium?

   (A) $(6,000 \div 3) + (600 \div 3) + (90 \div 3) + (3 \div 3) = \square$
   (B) $(6,000 \div 3) + (600 \div 3) + (90 \div 3) + (30 \div 3) = \square$
   (C) $(6,000 \div 3) + (60 \div 3) + (90 \div 3) + (3 \div 3) = \square$
   (D) $(6,000 \div 3) + (600 \div 3) + (900 \div 3) + (3 \div 3) = \square$

Test Tip

Use models or drawings to help when dividing.

4. Which array correctly represents 79 ÷ 5?

Divide Whole Numbers Using Strategies
Numbers and Operations in Base Ten

DIRECTIONS: Choose or write the correct answer.

> **Strategy**
> Remember how multiplication and division relate to help you solve division problems.

DIRECTIONS: Use the information below to answer Questions 5 and 6.

Remy solved the problem 672 ÷ 6. These are the steps she did to solve it.

- First, she found how many times 6 can go into 6 hundreds.

- Then, she found how many times 6 can go into 7 tens.

- Finally, she found how many times 6 can go into 2 ones.

5. Is Remy correct? Tell why or why not.

> **Test Tip**
> You can check your answers in a division problem by multiplying the quotient by the divisor.

8. Luis organizes books in the school library. He wants to place 135 books in equal stacks of 9 books each.

He does the division problem below to find how many books will be in each stack.

$$135 \div 9 = 15$$

Write an equation Luis can use to check his division.

6. Solve the problem. Show your work.

9. Look at the division problem below.

$$335 \div 5$$

Use words or numbers to explain how you can break apart 335 to make the division easier. Be sure to include the quotient in your explanation.

7. Jessie earned $574 for mowing his neighbor's lawn for 7 weeks during the summer. She earned the same amount each week. Which equation correctly shows how much money Jessie earned per week?

- Ⓐ 574 ÷ 7 = 820
- Ⓑ 574 ÷ 7 = 182
- Ⓒ 574 ÷ 7 = 82
- Ⓓ 574 ÷ 7 = 802

Find Equivalent Fractions
Numbers and Operations—Fractions

DIRECTIONS: Choose or write the correct answer.

Strategy Use drawings to understand data.

1. Nathan has two vegetable gardens he has divided
   into equal parts, as shown. Nathan planted
   carrots in the shaded parts. He says his garden
   plots show that $\frac{3}{4} = \frac{6}{8}$. Which is another way to
   show that the fractions are equal?

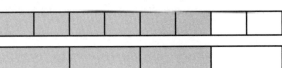

   Ⓐ $\frac{3}{4} \times \frac{2}{2}$

   Ⓑ $\frac{3}{4} + \frac{3}{4}$

   Ⓒ $\frac{3}{4} + \frac{2}{2}$

   Ⓓ $\frac{3}{4} \times \frac{2}{1}$

Test Tip

When drawings are presented in a problem,
look carefully at them, and be sure you
understand what they represent.

2. Alonzo is painting some sections of a board. He
   paints 1 part white, 1 part blue, and 1 part black.
   The shaded part of the picture shows the part of
   the board that is blue. Which fraction is
   equivalent to the part that is painted blue?
   Choose all that apply.

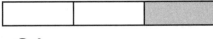

   Ⓐ $\frac{2}{6}$

   Ⓑ $\frac{1}{6}$

   Ⓒ $\frac{3}{9}$

   Ⓓ $\frac{4}{12}$

4. Write two fractions that have the same value
   as $\frac{1}{2}$. Explain how you know they have the
   same value.

   _____

   _____

   _____

5. Which model represents the same fractional
   amount as the model below? Choose all that apply.

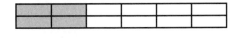

3. Jana and Farida each ate a whole small pizza.
   Jana's pizza is shown. Farida's pizza was the
   same size but was cut into more pieces, also all
   the same size. How many pieces might Farida's
   pizza have had? Show how you know.

Find Equivalent Fractions
Numbers and Operations—Fractions

DIRECTIONS: Choose or write the correct answer.

> **Strategy** Look at the shaded parts of drawings to understand the parts and the entire drawing to understand wholes.

6. Kenji drew Fraction Model A and Luis drew Fraction Model B. Both boys think their drawings represent equal fractions. Are they correct? Show why or why not.

A   B

_____

_____

_____

_____

7. Look at the shaded fraction model. Then, in the empty rectangle, draw a different model equivalent to the first one.

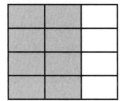 

8. Explain how you know the two fraction models in Question 7 are equivalent. Show your work.

9. Draw three equal-sized circles and shade fractions to show that:

$$\frac{1}{3} = \frac{2}{6} = \frac{4}{12}$$

> ## Test Tip
> Equivalent fractions can be created by multiplying both the numerator and denominator by the same number or by dividing a shaded region into various parts.

Compare Fractions
Numbers and Operations—Fractions

DIRECTIONS: Choose or write the correct answer.

Strategy Use fraction models to compare fractions with different numerators and denominators.

1. Look at the shaded parts. Which correctly compares the two fractions shown by the models? Choose all that apply.

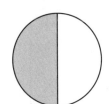 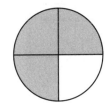

- (A) $\frac{1}{2} < \frac{3}{4}$
- (B) $\frac{1}{2} + \frac{3}{4}$
- (C) $\frac{3}{4} > \frac{1}{2}$
- (D) $\frac{1}{2} = \frac{3}{4}$

DIRECTIONS: Use the fraction models below to answer Questions 2 and 3.

Test Tip

Use models and drawings to help you visualize fractions.

2. Chaz used the models to compare two fractions. What two fractions did he compare?

_____

3. Write two number sentences comparing the fractions.

_____

DIRECTIONS: Use the information below to answer Questions 4–6.

> Joaquim and Fritz are each eating a medium pizza. Fritz's pizza has 3 slices. He eats 2 slices. Joaquim's pizza has 6 slices. He eats 4 slices. Who eats more pizza?

4. Write fractions to show the amount of pizza Joaquim and Fritz each eat.

_____

5. Draw on the two number lines below to compare the fractional amounts of pizza that Joaquim and Fritz eat.

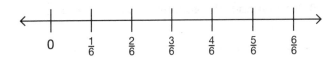

6. Write a number sentence to compare the fractional amounts of pizza Joaquim and Fritz eat.

_____

Compare Fractions
Numbers and Operations—Fractions

DIRECTIONS: Choose or write the correct answer.

Strategy   Rewrite the problem in your own words to answer the questions.

7. Which two fractions are equal to $\frac{3}{4}$?

(A) $\frac{7}{11}$

(B) $\frac{9}{12}$

(C) $\frac{4}{3}$

(D) $\frac{6}{8}$

8. Which fraction is equal to $\frac{2}{5}$?

(A) $\frac{5}{10}$

(B) $\frac{4}{15}$

(C) $\frac{6}{15}$

(D) $\frac{6}{20}$

9. Write a pair of fractions that shows that $\frac{2}{3} < \frac{7}{9}$.

_____

10. Is $\frac{2}{8}$ equal to $\frac{1}{2}$? Write how you know.

_____

_____

11. Write a number sentence comparing the two fractions represented by the fraction models below.

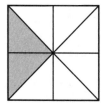 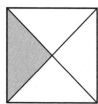

_____

Compose and Decompose Fractions
Numbers and Operations—Fractions

DIRECTIONS: Choose or write the correct answer.

Strategy | Compose and decompose fractions using addition.

1. **Which format shows the sum of $\frac{3}{4}$? Choose all that apply.**

   Ⓐ $\frac{1}{4} + \frac{1}{4} + \frac{1}{4}$

   Ⓑ $\frac{1}{4} + \frac{3}{4}$

   Ⓒ $\frac{1}{4} + \frac{2}{4}$

   Ⓓ $\frac{1}{4} + \frac{1}{4} + \frac{2}{4}$

2. **Which expression does not have a value of 1?**

   Ⓐ $\frac{7}{12} + \frac{5}{12}$

   Ⓑ $\frac{1}{12} + \frac{10}{12}$

   Ⓒ $\frac{4}{12} + \frac{8}{12}$

   Ⓓ $\frac{1}{12} + \frac{1}{12} + \frac{10}{12}$

Test Tip

Pay close attention to the numbers in the problem and the answer choices. If you misread even one number, you may choose the wrong answer.

3. **Lacy drew the fraction model below to help her add fractions. Write the equation shown by her model.**

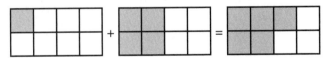

   _____

DIRECTIONS: Use the mixed number $4\frac{3}{4}$ to answer Questions 4 and 5.

4. **Show two ways to decompose the mixed number.**

5. **Choose one way you decomposed the mixed number in Question 4, and draw a model to prove it is equal to $4\frac{3}{4}$.**

6. **Lyla has some hair clips, and $\frac{2}{3}$ of them are blue. Which expression or fraction model shows $\frac{2}{3}$? Choose all that apply.**

   Ⓐ $\frac{1}{3} + \frac{1}{3}$

   Ⓑ

   Ⓒ $\frac{1}{3} + \frac{2}{3}$

   Ⓓ

Compose and Decompose Fractions
Numbers and Operations—Fractions

DIRECTIONS: Choose or write the correct answer.

Strategy Use visuals when composing and decomposing fractions. Draw boxes to equal the denominator. Then, shade in boxes that equal the numerator. Use different colors for each fraction.

Test Tip When decomposing fractions using addition, use the same denominator.

7. **Which is a correct way to write $1\frac{6}{8}$ as a sum of fractions?**

    Ⓐ $\frac{8}{8} + \frac{8}{8} + \frac{8}{8} + \frac{8}{8} + \frac{8}{8} + \frac{8}{8} + \frac{1}{1}$

    Ⓑ $\frac{8}{8} + \frac{1}{8} + \frac{5}{8}$

    Ⓒ $\frac{6}{8} + \frac{1}{8}$

    Ⓓ $\frac{8}{8} + \frac{6}{6}$

Test Tip

Before you choose an answer, ask yourself, "Does this answer make sense?"

8. **Jerrod shaded a shape as shown below.**

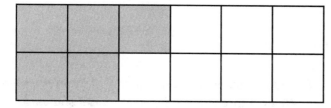

    Write three number sentences to show how Jerrod shaded the shape.

    _____

    _____

    _____

9. **Look at the equation below. Draw and shade a model to show the equation.**

    $$\frac{1}{8} + \frac{4}{8} = \frac{5}{8}$$

    ☐☐☐☐ + ☐☐☐☐ = ☐☐☐☐

10. **Which is the correct way to write $\frac{2}{18} + \frac{15}{18} + \frac{1}{18}$? Choose all that apply.**

    Ⓐ $\frac{18}{18}$

    Ⓑ 1

    Ⓒ $\frac{17}{18}$

    Ⓓ $\frac{16}{18}$

11. $\frac{3}{4} - \frac{2}{4} =$ _____

12. $\frac{1}{6} + \frac{3}{6} + \frac{1}{6} =$ _____

Add and Subtract Mixed Numbers
Numbers and Operations—Fractions

DIRECTIONS: Choose or write the correct answer.

> **Strategy** Use equivalent fractions to add and subtract mixed numbers with like denominators.

1. Which is the sum of $1\frac{2}{4} + 2\frac{1}{4}$?

   (A) $\frac{3}{4}$

   (B) $3\frac{3}{4}$

   (C) $2\frac{3}{4}$

   (D) $1\frac{3}{4}$

2. The Spencer family went on a trip. It took them $1\frac{1}{6}$ hours the first day and $2\frac{4}{6}$ hours the next day to get to their destination. What is the total time for their trip? Show your work.

3. Bianca has $3\frac{4}{8}$ pizzas left over from her party. She takes some pizza to her friend's house the next day and leaves $1\frac{3}{8}$ pizzas at home. How much pizza did Bianca take to her friend's house?

   (A) $2\frac{1}{8}$ pizzas

   (B) $4\frac{7}{8}$ pizzas

   (C) $\frac{1}{8}$ pizza

   (D) $1\frac{1}{8}$ pizza

4. Look at the equation below.

   $$1\frac{2}{3} - \frac{1}{3} = n$$

   What is true about n in the following number sentences? Choose all that apply.

   (A) $\frac{5}{3} - \frac{1}{3} = n$

   (B) $n + \frac{1}{3} = 1\frac{2}{3}$

   (C) $n - 1\frac{2}{3} = \frac{1}{3}$

   (D) $n = \frac{4}{3}$

> **Test Tip**
> Look carefully at every answer choice. Then, choose the one that best answers the problem.

5. Add. Show your work.

   $$4\frac{2}{6} + 3\frac{2}{6}$$

Add and Subtract Mixed Numbers
Numbers and Operations—Fractions

DIRECTIONS: Choose or write the correct answer.

Strategy   Use addition and subtraction of mixed numbers with like denominators to solve real-world problems.

6. Raj wants to solve this number sentence, but he doesn't know where to begin.

$$2\frac{4}{12} - \frac{7}{12} = \square$$

Use words or numbers to help Raj solve the problem. Include the difference in your explanation.

7. Inga had $2\frac{3}{4}$ granola bars. She ate $\frac{2}{4}$ of them at snack time. How much was left for her to eat after school? Show your work.

8. Rachel is making doll clothes for her younger sister's doll. She has a total of $4\frac{5}{8}$ yards of cloth. She uses $1\frac{3}{8}$ yards to make dresses and $\frac{4}{8}$ yard to make pants. How much cloth does she have left to make shirts? Show how you found your answer.

9. Dominic was watering the school garden. He started with 8 gallons of water. He used $3\frac{3}{4}$ gallons to water the tomatoes and $2\frac{1}{4}$ gallons to water the sunflowers. How many gallons of water did he have left? Show your work.

10. Nico needs 5 cups of flour for his bread recipe. He only has $3\frac{1}{4}$ cups of flour. How much more flour does Nico need? Show how you found your answer.

Multiply a Fraction by a Whole Number
Numbers and Operations—Fractions

DIRECTIONS: Choose or write the correct answer.

> **Strategy**   Use multiplication of a whole number and a fraction to solve the problems.

1. Jason measured the total length of 8 boards. Each board is $\frac{1}{4}$ meter long. What is the total length of Jason's boards?

   (A) 32 meters

   (B) $8\frac{1}{4}$ meters

   (C) 2 meters

   (D) $7\frac{3}{4}$ meters

> ## Test Tip
> When multiplying a fraction by a whole number, be sure you multiply the numerator of the fraction by the whole number. Then, place the product above the denominator.

2. What is $3 \times \frac{2}{5}$?

   (A) $\frac{5}{5}$

   (B) $1\frac{1}{5}$

   (C) $3\frac{2}{5}$

   (D) $\frac{54}{100}$

3. Charlotte bought $\frac{5}{8}$ pound of turkey on Monday to make sandwiches. On Thursday, she ran out of turkey, so she bought 3 times as much as she bought on Monday. How much turkey did Charlotte buy on Thursday? Show your work.

4. Mrs. Lopez is sewing letters on the baseball team's uniforms. It takes her $\frac{1}{5}$ hour to finish one uniform. How much time will it take her to sew letters on 9 uniforms?

   (A) $1\frac{4}{5}$ hours

   (B) $9\frac{1}{5}$ hours

   (C) 2 hours

   (D) $\frac{5}{9}$ hour

5. A recipe calls for $\frac{3}{4}$ cup flour. Janelle wants to make 3 times the recipe. Which equation can be used to find how much flour Janelle needs? Choose all that apply.

   (A) $3 \times \frac{3}{4} = \square$

   (B) $\frac{3}{4} + \frac{3}{4} + \frac{3}{4} = \square$

   (C) $3 + \frac{3}{4} = \square$

   (D) $3 + 3 + 3 + \frac{3}{4} = \square$

6. Solve the problem in Question 5. Show the equation you used to solve the problem.

Multiply a Fraction by a Whole Number
Numbers and Operations—Fractions

DIRECTIONS: Choose or write the correct answer.

Strategy   Use visual fraction models, such as number lines, to help you multiply a fraction by a whole number.

7. Roberto practices running every day after school. His running path is $\frac{2}{3}$ mile long. How many miles does he run at the end of 5 days? Show your work.

8. Justin's basketball team set a record when they scored 99 points in one game. Justin scored $\frac{1}{3}$ of the points, and Levon scored $\frac{1}{9}$ of the points. How many more points did Justin score than Levon?

_____

_____

9. Liza's teacher asked her to show that $\frac{3}{8}$ is the same as $3 \times \frac{1}{8}$. Draw a picture to show how Liza might have shown this.

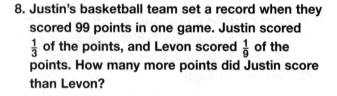

DIRECTIONS: Use the information below to answer Questions 10 and 11.

Amrita is making special sauce to serve with the meal she is making. She wants to make seven $\frac{1}{4}$-cup servings.

10. Draw a number line below to show how many total cups of sauce Amrita needs to make.

11. Write an equation and solve it to show how to find how many total cups of sauce Amrita needs to make.

_____

12. Emilio spent $\frac{4}{6}$ hour every day last week practicing his guitar. Write an equation to show how many hours total, *h*, Emilio spent practicing. Then, solve it.

_____

_____

Math

Change Fractions with Denominators of 10 to Equivalent Fractions with Denominators of 100

Numbers and Operations—Fractions

DIRECTIONS: Choose or write the correct answer.

Strategy Use a tenths grid and a hundredths grid to find equivalent fractions.

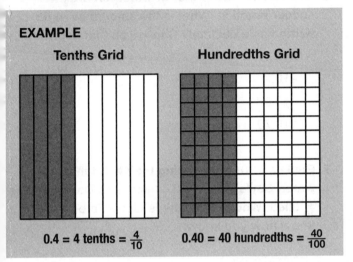

EXAMPLE

Tenths Grid   Hundredths Grid

$0.4 = 4$ tenths $= \frac{4}{10}$ $0.40 = 40$ hundredths $= \frac{40}{100}$

1. Which fraction is equivalent to $\frac{90}{100}$?

  Ⓐ $\frac{9}{10}$

  Ⓑ $\frac{9}{100}$

  Ⓒ $\frac{19}{100}$

  Ⓓ $\frac{9}{1}$

2. What is the sum of $\frac{5}{10}$ and $\frac{4}{100}$?

  Ⓐ $\frac{9}{10}$

  Ⓑ $\frac{54}{110}$

  Ⓒ $\frac{9}{100}$

  Ⓓ $\frac{54}{100}$

3. Yao shaded $\frac{3}{10}$ of a piece of grid paper. Melanie shaded 64 hundredths of the same piece of grid paper. What is the total amount of grid paper that Yao and Melanie shaded? Write your answer as a decimal and a fraction. Show your work.

4. Mrs. Chang bought 0.57 kilogram of fruit. She already had 0.35 kilogram of fruit at home. What is the total weight of Mrs. Chang's fruit? Choose all that apply.

  Ⓐ $\frac{92}{100}$ kilogram

  Ⓑ $\frac{92}{10}$ kilogram

  Ⓒ 0.92 kilogram

  Ⓓ 9.02 kilogram

Test Tip

When adding two fractions, they must have the same denominator.

5. Isabel measured the rainfall for two weeks.

During Week 1, it rained $\frac{2}{10}$ inch.

During Week 2, it rained $\frac{4}{100}$ inch.

What is the total rainfall that Isabel measured for two weeks?

_____

Use Decimal Notation for Fractions
Numbers and Operations—Fractions

DIRECTIONS: Choose or write the correct answer.

Strategy Draw a place value chart to determine decimal equivalents.

EXAMPLE

You can use a place value chart to write decimals.

$\frac{43}{100}$ is read as "forty-three hundredths." It is written as 0.43.

$\frac{5}{10}$ is read as "five tenths." It is written as 0.5 or 0.50.

Hundreds	Tens	Ones	.	Tenths	Hundredths
		0	.	4	3
		0	.	5	0

1. Which decimal is equivalent to $\frac{67}{100}$?

   Ⓐ 0.76
   Ⓑ 1.67
   Ⓒ 0.67
   Ⓓ 0.7

DIRECTIONS: For Questions 2–5, change each decimal to a fraction.

2. 0.63 _____

3. 0.4 _____

4. 0.81 _____

5. 0.3 _____

6. Ava's bottle has $\frac{7}{10}$ liter of water left after her soccer practice. What is the amount of water written as a decimal? Choose all that apply.

   Ⓐ 0.107
   Ⓑ 0.7
   Ⓒ 0.07
   Ⓓ 0.70

7. Gayle and Doro are filling their fish tanks with water. Gayle's tank is 0.5 filled, and Doro's tank is $\frac{6}{10}$ filled. Whose fish tank is closer to being filled? Show how you know.

Test Tip

When reading decimals, the decimal point should be read as "and."

8. Look at the number line below. Mark these decimals on the line.

   0.35   0.89

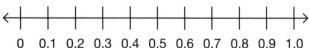

Compare Decimals
Numbers and Operations—Fractions

DIRECTIONS: Choose or write the correct answer.

Strategy   Compare decimals to answer questions.

DIRECTIONS: Use the table below to answer Questions 1 and 2.

Student	Height (meters)
Rachel	1.49
Alonzo	1.09
Maddie	1.5
Kira	1.7
Van	1.65

1. Which student is the tallest?

Ⓐ Van

Ⓑ Kira

Ⓒ Alonzo

Ⓓ Rachel

2. Which students' height measurements correctly complete this number sentence? Write their names on the line.

_____ > 1.5 meters

3. Which decimal correctly completes the number sentence?

2.4 < _____

Ⓐ 2.40

Ⓑ 2.44

Ⓒ 2.39

Ⓓ 2.04

4. Shade in the decimal models to show that 0.6 > 0.4.

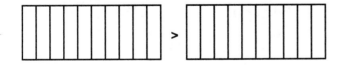

Test Tip

Be sure the whole numbers are the same when you compare decimals.

5. Look at the two decimal models below. Write a number sentence using <, >, or = to compare the pair of decimals.

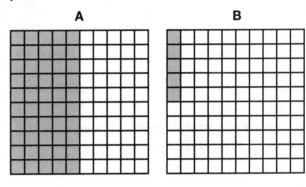

A   B

_____

DIRECTIONS: Use the following information to answer Questions 6 and 7.

Two farmers are comparing the amount of land they plant with corn. Farmer A plants corn on 0.85 of his land. Farmer B plants corn on 0.8 of his land.

6. Which farmer has a greater part of his land planted with corn? Explain how you know.

7. Write a number sentence using <, >, or = to support your answer in Question 6.

_____

Understand Measurement Units
Measurement

DIRECTIONS: Choose or write the correct answer.

Strategy   Use charts to help you find the equivalent measurements.

Equivalent Metric Measures		
Units of Length	**Units of Capacity**	**Units of Mass**
100 centimeters (cm) = 1 meter (m) 1,000 meters = 1 kilometer (km)	1 liter (L) = 1,000 milliliters (mL)	1 kilogram (kg) = 1,000 grams (g)

Equivalent Customary Measures		
Units of Length	**Units of Weight**	**Units of Time**
1 foot (ft.) = 12 inches (in.) 1 yard (yd.) = 3 feet	1 pound (lb.) = 16 ounces (oz.)	1 hour (hr.) = 60 minutes (min.) 1 minute = 60 seconds (sec.)

DIRECTIONS: Fill in the blanks with the equivalent measurement for Questions 1–6.

1. 7 yards = _____ feet

2. 24 inches = _____ feet

3. 160 ounces = _____ pounds

4. 15 pounds = _____ ounces

5. 10 kilograms = _____ grams

6. 5,000 grams = _____ kilograms

Test Tip

The metric system is based on multiples of 10.

7. Lucinda wants to run in a 10,000-meter race. The furthest Lucinda has ever run is $\frac{1}{2}$ that distance. In kilometers, what is the greatest distance Lucinda has ever run before?

Ⓐ 5 km

Ⓑ 10 km

Ⓒ 50 km

Ⓓ 1,000 km

Understand Measurement Units
Measurement

DIRECTIONS: Choose or write the correct answer.

8. Amelia climbed 2.5 meters up a ladder. How many centimeters is this?

_____

9. Which of the following equals 2,000 meters?

   (A) 200 km

   (B) 0.2 km

   (C) 20 km

   (D) 2 km

10. A football is 11 inches in length. How many footballs would have to be placed end to end to equal more than 1 yard? Show how you know.

Test Tip

You can use scratch paper to draw pictures or do your calculations.

11. On a baseball diamond, there are 4 bases. It is 90 feet between each base. Suppose a player hits a double and has reached second base. How much farther, in yards, does the player have to run to reach home? (Hint: Consider home the fourth base.) Show your work.

DIRECTIONS: Write the best unit of measure for questions 12–14.

12. It will take Lila 15 _____ to walk to her mailbox.

_____

13. Kayla's little sister is 96 _____ tall.

_____

14. Mr. Halinian drove 12 _____ to work each day.

_____

Solve Problems: Distance, Time, Volume, Mass, and Money
Measurement

DIRECTIONS: Choose or write the correct answer.

> ## Strategy
> Use addition, subtraction, and multiplication to solve real-world problems about various measurements.

1. If you burn 318 calories in 60 minutes playing basketball, how many calories would you burn in 30 minutes?

   (A) 636

   (B) 258

   (C) 288

   (D) 159

2. Arnell buys 3 books. Each book costs $4.25. He pays with a $20 bill. How much change does Arnell get?

   (A) $4.75

   (B) $11.50

   (C) $7.25

   (D) $17.00

3. A factory has 315 workers. One week, each worker received a $50 bonus. How much total bonus, *b*, did the workers receive? Write and solve an equation.

   _____

   _____

4. Barb used 8 quarts of water to wash her hands and face. How many pints of water did Barb use? Show your work.

> ## Test Tip
> Read each problem carefully and make sure you understand what is being asked.

5. Jesse bought a pack of baseball cards for $3.50 and 2 packs of football cards for $4.50 each. He has $5.89 left over. How much money did Jessie start with? Show your work.

6. Travis started his homework at 6:56 p.m. and finished at 8:34 p.m. How long did he spend doing homework?

   (A) 1 hr. 38 mins.

   (B) 1 hr. 42 mins.

   (C) 1 hr. 26 mins.

   (D) 1 hr. 36 mins.

Solve Problems: Distance, Time, Volume, Mass, and Money
Measurement

DIRECTIONS: Choose or write the correct answer.

Strategy Look for key words, numbers, and figures in each problem to be sure you perform the correct operation.

7. Chloe's school day lasts 7 hours and 45 minutes. If school starts at 8:20, what time does it end?

_____

8. A small hair comb has a mass of 35 grams. How many milligrams does that equal?

_____

9. Monica drank $\frac{3}{8}$ of her juice for lunch and $\frac{2}{8}$ of it for her afterschool snack. Ricky drank $\frac{2}{6}$ of his juice drink for lunch and $\frac{1}{6}$ of it for his afterschool snack. Each drink can holds 24 ounces. Who drank more of their fruit juice? How much more? Show your work.

10. A football field is 100 yards long. How many inches is that?

  (A) 1,200 inches

  (B) 360 inches

  (C) 3,600 inches

  (D) 120 inches

11. Tia uses a 1-quart container to fill her 10-gallon fish tank. How many times must she fill the 1-quart container with water to fill the fish tank? Show how you know.

12. Lindsay poured an equal amount of lemonade into 2 glasses from a 1-liter bottle. She had 510 milliliters of lemonade left after pouring the two glasses. How much lemonade did Lindsay pour into each glass?

  (A) 245 milliliters

  (B) 510 milliliters

  (C) 500 milliliters

  (D) 755 milliliters

Solve Problems: Area
Measurement and Data

DIRECTIONS: Choose or write the correct answer.

> ## Strategy   Draw and label rectangles to answer questions about area.

EXAMPLE

The area of a figure is the number of square units a figure covers.

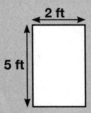

2 ft

5 ft

You can use a formula to find the area

$A = l \times w$

$A = 5 \times 2 = 10$

The area is 10 square feet.

1. What is the area of the rectangle?

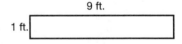

9 ft.

1 ft.

- (A) 10 square ft.
- (B) 9 square ft.
- (C) 20 square ft.
- (D) 18 square ft.

> ## Test Tip
>
> Remember, the answer for area will always be in square units.

DIRECTIONS: Use the rectangles below to answer Questions 2 and 3.

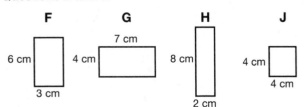

F   G   H   J

7 cm

6 cm   4 cm   8 cm   4 cm

3 cm   2 cm   4 cm

2. Which two rectangles have the same area?

_____

3. Which rectangle has the greatest area? Show how you know.

4. Josh has a picture with an area of 45 square inches. He wants to paste his picture on a page in his scrapbook that measures 9 inches in length and 6 inches in width. Will his picture fit on the page? Write how you know.

5. The area of a park is 16 square miles. The length of the park is 8 miles. What is the perimeter of the park?

- (A) 20 miles
- (B) 24 miles
- (C) 32 miles
- (D) 64 miles

Solve Problems: Perimeter
Measurement and Data

DIRECTIONS: Choose or write the correct answer.

Strategy   Draw and label rectangles to answer questions about perimeter.

EXAMPLE

Perimeter is the distance around the edge of a shape.

Width = 5 ft.

Length = 18 ft.

You can use a formula to find the perimeter.

$P = 2l + 2w$ or $2 (l + w)$

$P = 2 \times 18 + 2 \times 5 =$

$P = 36 + 10 = 46$

The perimeter is 46 feet.

1. **A rectangle has a length of 15 feet and a width of 3 feet. What is the perimeter?**

   (A) 30 feet

   (B) 21 feet

   (C) 36 feet

   (D) 33 feet

Test Tip

Another way to find the perimeter is to add the lengths of the four sides.

DIRECTIONS: Use the rectangles below to answer Questions 2 and 3.

A

B

C

D

5 cm □ 5 cm

4 cm [7 cm]

8 cm [2 cm]

6 cm [3 cm]

2. **Which two rectangles have the same perimeter?**

   _____

3. **Which rectangle has the greatest perimeter? Show how you know.**

4. **The perimeter of the rectangle is 48 feet. The length is 15 feet. What is the width of the rectangle? Show how you found your answer.**

   Length = 15 ft.

5. **Check your answer to Question 4 by putting numbers into the formula $P = 2l + 2w$.**

Make a Line Plot and Solve Problems
Measurement and Data

DIRECTIONS: Choose or write the correct answer.

Strategy   Use line plots to understand data and solve problems.

DIRECTIONS: Use the line plot below to answer Questions 1–3.

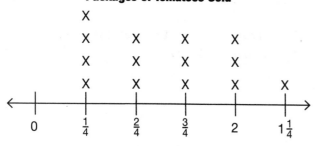

Key: X = 1 package

Packages of Tomatoes Sold

Weight (pounds)

DIRECTIONS: Use the line plot to answer questions 4–5.

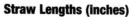

Straw Lengths (inches)

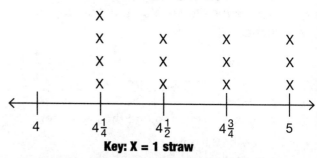

Key: X = 1 straw

1. **What is the difference in the total pounds of tomatoes sold in the 2-pound packages and the $\frac{1}{4}$-pound packages?**

   Ⓐ $2\frac{1}{4}$ pounds

   Ⓑ $\frac{3}{4}$ pound

   Ⓒ 5 pounds

   Ⓓ 2 pounds

2. **What is the total number of pounds of tomatoes sold in $\frac{1}{2}$-pound packages?**

   Ⓐ $2\frac{1}{2}$ pounds

   Ⓑ $1\frac{1}{2}$ pounds

   Ⓒ 3 pounds

   Ⓓ 1 pound

3. **What is the total amount of tomatoes sold in packages less than $\frac{3}{4}$ pound? Show your work.**

Test Tip

The first and last measures on a line plot should be the greatest and least values in the data.

4. **Lavita is making a picture by pasting straws on a large piece of paper. She cut the straws into different lengths. If she puts the shortest straws end to end, how long will the length of straws be?**

   Ⓐ 16 inches

   Ⓑ $16\frac{1}{4}$ inches

   Ⓒ 17 inches

   Ⓓ $12\frac{3}{4}$ inches

5. **What is the difference in length between the shortest and longest straws? Show how you know.**

Understand Angle Concepts and Measurement
Measurement and Data

DIRECTIONS: Choose or write the correct answer.

> ## Strategy
> Use drawings or sketches to answer questions about angle measurement.

1. Levi used a map to get from the Computer Center to the Mathematics Building at the city college. Which is the best estimate of the measure of the angle formed by the two streets?

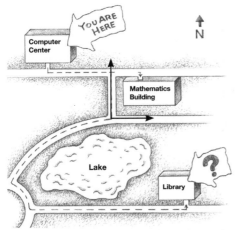

(A) 90°

(B) 180°

(C) 55°

(D) 102°

DIRECTIONS: Use ray *AB* below to answer Questions 2–4.

2. Draw and label ray *AC* so that rays *AC* and *AB* form angle *CAB* that is greater than 90°.

3. Draw and label ray *AD* so that rays *AD* and *AB* form angle *DAB* that is less than 90°.

4. Draw and label ray *AF* so that rays *AC* and *AF* form angle *CAF* that is greater than 180°.

DIRECTIONS: Use the information below to answer Questions 5 and 6.

> ## Test Tip
> A circle is 360°.

Ryan runs around a circular track every day after school. When he is three-fourths of the way around the track, he says he has run 270° around the track.

5. Is Ryan correct?

6. Show how you know by drawing on the circle below.

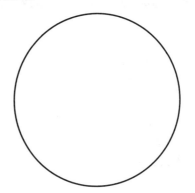

Measuring Angles
Geometry

DIRECTIONS: Choose or write the correct answer.

Strategy   Use a protractor to answer questions about angle measurement.

EXAMPLE

You can use a protractor to measure angles.

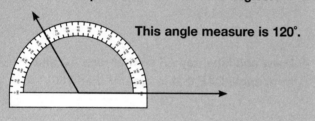

This angle measure is 120°.

1. Which measurement is closest to the degree measurement of this angle?

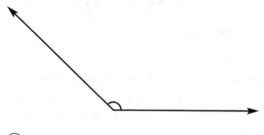

(A) 200°

(B) 135°

(C) 45°

(D) 90°

2. What is the measure of angle *ABC*?

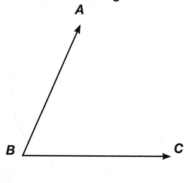

_____

3. Mei drew an angle less than 60°. Which could be the angle Mei drew? Choose all that apply.

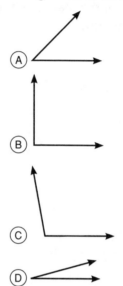

Test Tip

Protractors usually have two sets of numbers going in opposite directions. Be careful which sets you use.

DIRECTIONS: Use a protractor to measure the angles in questions 4 and 5.

4. This angle measures _____.

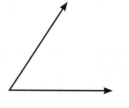

5. This angle measures _____.

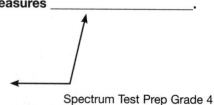

Solve Problems: Unknown Angle Measures
Geometry

DIRECTIONS: Choose or write the correct answer.

Strategy Solve unknown measures by using the properties of angles.

EXAMPLE

The angle measures in a triangle always equal 180°. The angle measures in any quadrilateral always equal 360°.

What is the measure of angle *A*?

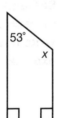

Answer: The measure is 60 degrees because 180 – (30 + 90) = 60.

Test Tip

The angle measure of the whole is the sum of the angle measures of all the parts.

DIRECTIONS: Use the figures below to answer questions 3 and 4.

Figure A   **Figure B**

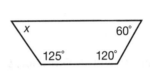   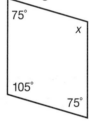

1. **Which is the measure of angle *X*?**

    Ⓐ 180°

    Ⓑ 360°

    Ⓒ 127°

    Ⓓ 307°

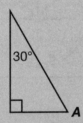

3. **Without doing the calculation, in which figure is the measure of angle *x* greater? Write how you know.**

    _____

    _____

    _____

    _____

    _____

    _____

2. **What is the measure of angle *X*? Write how you know. Use an equation in your answer.**

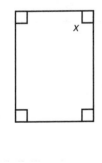 

4. **Write the measure of each angle *x*. Show your work.**

Solve Problems: Unknown Angle Measures
Geometry

DIRECTIONS: Choose or write the correct answer.

> **Strategy** Use the drawings and labels to understand which angle measurement to find.

DIRECTIONS: Use the image below to answer Questions 5 and 6.

5. What is the measure of angle *H*?

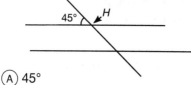

- (A) 45°
- (B) 180°
- (C) 135°
- (D) 65°

6. Write how you found your answer in Question 5.

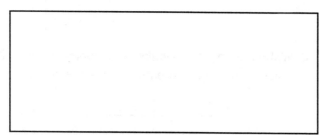

> **Test Tip**
> The sum of the angles of a circle is 360°.

7. At 3:00, the hands on the clock form a 90° angle. What angle will they be at 6:00?

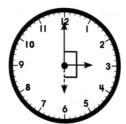

- (A) 360°   (C) 108°
- (B) 180°   (D) 90°

8. Leo cut his pizza into 8 equal parts. He noticed that 2 pieces form a 90° angle. What is the measure of each piece of pizza? Show how you know.

9. Sarita used this spinner in a game. What is the measure of the angle marked on the spinner? Write how you know. Use an equation in your explanation.

Identify Lines and Angles
Geometry

DIRECTIONS: Choose or write the correct answer.

Strategy Use the properties of lines and angles to answer the questions.

EXAMPLE

This shape has 2 acute angles and 2 obtuse angles. It has one pair of parallel lines.

1. Which is an obtuse angle? Choose all that apply.

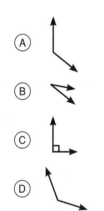

(A)

(B)

(C)

(D)

2. Which is a line segment?

(A) •————•

(B) •————▶

(C) ◀•———•▶

(D)

3. What point is on both the circle and the square?

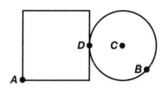

Test Tip

Remember, a point is a position on a plane.

4. Which is a ray?

(A) ◀•————▶

(B) •————•

(C) •

(D) •————▶

Math

Solve Problems: Unknown Angle Measures
Geometry

DIRECTIONS: Choose or write the correct answer.

> ## Strategy
> Use what you know about the types of angles and their measurements to solve unknown measures.

DIRECTIONS: Use the shape below to answer questions 1–5.

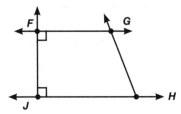

1. Name the angles that appear to be right angles.

   _____

2. Name an obtuse angle.

   _____

3. Name an acute angle.

   _____

4. Name a pair of perpendicular lines.

   _____

   _____

5. Name a pair of parallel lines.

   _____

   _____

> ## Test Tip
> Remember, *parallel* describes lines that do not and will never intersect.

DIRECTIONS: Use the clocks below to answer questions 6–8.

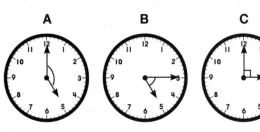

6. Which clock shows a right angle between the hour and minute hands?

   _____

7. Which clock shows an obtuse angle between the hour and minute hands?

   _____

8. Which clock shows an acute angle between the hour and minute hands?

   _____

Classify Two-Dimensional Figures
Geometry

DIRECTIONS: Choose or write the correct answer.

Strategy   Use the properties of two-dimensional figures to solve problems.

EXAMPLE

Two-dimensional figures can be classified based on the presence or absence of parallel or perpendicular lines or the presence or absence of angles of a certain size.

EXAMPLE

This figure is a trapezoid. One pair of opposite sides is parallel. It has no perpendicular lines. It has no right angles.

This figure is a rectangle. Two pairs of opposite sides are parallel. It has perpendicular lines. It has 4 right angles.

1. What is true about all of these triangles?

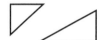

- Ⓐ They all have 3 obtuse angles.
- Ⓑ They all have right angles.
- Ⓒ They all have 3 acute angles.
- Ⓓ They all have 1 right, 1 obtuse, and 1 acute angle.

2. Which triangle appears to be a right triangle?

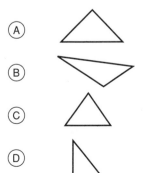

- Ⓐ
- Ⓑ
- Ⓒ
- Ⓓ

3. Paulo says that both of these shapes have parallel and perpendicular lines. Is Paulo correct? Write how you know.

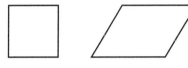

_____

_____

_____

Test Tip

Remember, two lines are parallel if they never intersect and are always an equal distance from each other. Two lines are perpendicular if they intersect at right angles.

4. Jaime wants to place the shapes below into two groups. One group has shapes with acute angles. The other group has shapes with obtuse angles. Which shapes will Jaime put in both groups? Write how you know.

  A   B   C   D

_____

_____

_____

_____

Classify Two-Dimensional Figures
Geometry

DIRECTIONS: Choose or write the correct answer.

> ## Strategy
> Draw a picture and use the properties of lines and angles to describe it.

DIRECTIONS: Use the information and shapes below to answer questions 5 and 6.

5. **In the space below, use any combination of these basic shapes to create a drawing of a person, place, or thing.**

6. **Describe the picture you drew. Use terms such as acute angle, obtuse angle, right angle, parallel lines, and perpendicular lines in your description.**

Identify Symmetry
Geometry

DIRECTIONS: Choose or write the correct answer.

Strategy   Use the properties of symmetry to answer questions.

EXAMPLE

An object or shape has a line of symmetry when the two sides can be folded along a line and match perfectly. Each side is a mirror image of the other. For example:

This rhombus has two lines of symmetry.    This arrow has one line of symmetry.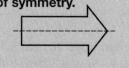

1. Which figure below does NOT show a line of symmetry?

Ⓐ

Ⓑ

Ⓒ

Ⓓ

2. Look at the letters below. Which two do not have a line of symmetry?

Ⓐ **O**

Ⓑ **P**

Ⓒ **X**

Ⓓ **G**

Test Tip

Folding cut-out figures will help you determine whether a figure has one or more lines of symmetry.

3. Henry said if he folded the figure below in half, it would have a line of symmetry. Is Henry correct? Show why or why not.

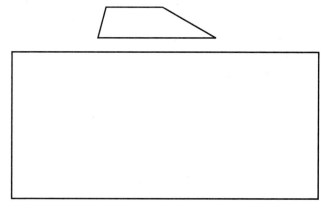

4. Draw all the lines of symmetry on this figure. Then, write how many lines of symmetry it has.

Strategy Review
Math

In this section, you will review the strategies you learned and apply them to practice the skills.

Strategy — Look for key words in word problems that help you determine which operation to use.

EXAMPLE

Eli's favorite macaroni and cheese recipes uses $\frac{5}{8}$ of a pound of cheese for the sauce and another $\frac{2}{8}$ of a pound shredded and sprinkled on top. How much cheese did Eli use altogether? If Eli started with 1 pound of cheese, how much is left? Show your work.

First, identify key words that tell you what operations to use.

The word "altogether" suggests addition.

The word "left" suggests subtraction.

Then, write and solve an equation to show how much Eli used.

$\frac{5}{8} + \frac{2}{8} = \frac{7}{8}$ pound of cheese used.

Then, write and solve an equation to show how much Eli has left.

$1 - \frac{7}{8} = \frac{8}{8} - \frac{7}{8} = \frac{1}{8}$ pound of cheese left.

1. Rory poured an equal amount of cider into 3 cups from a 2-liter jug. He had 1,100 milliliters of cider left after pouring the 3 cups. How much cider did Rory pour into each cup?

(A) 266 milliliters

(B) 300 milliliters

(C) 366 milliliters

(D) 400 milliliters

Explain what operations you used, and identify the key words that helped you choose those operations.

_____

_____

_____

_____

2. Sophie buys 2 t-shirts. Each t-shirt costs $6.75. She pays with a $20 bill. How much change does Sophie get back?

(A) $6.50

(B) $6.75

(C) $7.50

(D) $7.75

Explain what operations you used, and identify the key words that helped you choose those operations.

_____

_____

_____

_____

_____

Strategy Review
Math

| **Strategy** | Use drawings, graphs, or number lines to understand and solve a problem. |

EXAMPLE

Mariah is fencing her garden to keep bunnies from eating the vegetables. She has 45 feet of fencing. The sides of the garden are 15 feet, 5 feet, 15 feet, and 5 feet. Does Mariah have enough fencing to go all of the way around her garden? Write or draw a picture to show how you know.

First, draw a picture to help visualize the problem.

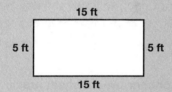

Then, find the perimeter of the garden by adding its sides.

15 + 5 + 15 + 5 = 40 feet

Now, compare the amount of fence with the perimeter.

Since 40 feet is less than 45 feet, she has enough fencing.

1. Chris built a sandbox that measures 6 feet by 8 feet. He wants to expand the sandbox so that it is a square. What will be the area of his new sandbox? Draw a picture to help you choose the correct answer.

   (A) 36 square feet

   (B) 48 square feet

   (C) 64 square feet

   (D) 72 square feet

2. Rowan wants to make a 1-foot wide rectangular path around his vegetable garden. The rectangular garden has a length of 4 feet and a width of 3 feet. What will be the area of the path? Draw a picture to help you find the correct answer.

_____

_____

_____

_____

Strategy Review
Math

> **Strategy** | Organize and display data to interpret them.

EXAMPLE

A tea shop tracks the sizes of cups of tea ordered. On Tuesday morning, customers order the following sizes:

small, small, medium, small, large, large, large, medium, medium, large, large, medium

Use a line plot to organize the data.

First, label the line plot with the range of data.

Then, add X's to show the data.

```
                              X
                 X            X
    X            X            X
    X            X            X
    X            X            X
  _____
    small       medium       large
```

Now, you can use your line plot to answer questions about the data.

1. How many people ordered cups of tea?
   Answer: 12

2. What size tea was ordered most often?
   Answer: large

3. What size tea was ordered least often?
   Answer: small

EXAMPLE

A food cart sells 29 sandwiches at lunch on Monday. Nine of the sandwiches are ham. Nineteen of the sandwiches are turkey. The rest of the sandwiches are vegetarian. The food cart also sells 25 bags of chips and 34 drinks. How many vegetarian sandwiches did the food cart sell?

What is the given information?

A food cart sells 29 sandwiches at lunch on Monday. Nine of the sandwiches are ham. Nineteen of the sandwiches are turkey. The rest of the sandwiches are vegetarian. The food cart also sells 25 bags of chips and 34 drinks.

What are you being asked to find?

the number of vegetarian sandwiches sold

Is any of the given information extra, or not needed?

Yes, we do not need to know the day, time, number of bags of chips, or number of drinks sold.

1. A music teacher orders sheet music for each student in her class. There are 34 students in the class. She places 4 pieces of music in each student's folder. The folders cost $1.95 each. How many pieces of sheet music did the teacher order? *What is the given information?*

_____

_____

_____

_____

_____

_____

What are you being asked to find?

_____

Is any of the given information extra, or not needed?

_____

_____

Strategy Review
Math

EXAMPLE

Jackson painted a door that was 8 feet by 3 feet. Use the formula for area, $A = l \times w$, to find the area of the door Jackson painted.

First, write the formula for the area of rectangle.

$A = l \times w$

Put the measurements into the formula.

$A = l \times w = 8 \times 3 = 24$

The area of the wall is 24 square feet.

1. A path through Walt's garden is 30 feet long and 4 feet wide. What is the area of the path? Show your work.

2. Rectangle A has a length of 5 centimeters and a width of 2 centimeters. What is the area of Rectangle A?

   (A) 7 cm

   (B) 10 cm

   (C) 7 square cm

   (D) 10 square cm

Rectangle B has a length of 4 centimeters and a width of 3 centimeters. What is the area of Rectangle B?

_____

Is Rectangle A larger or smaller than Rectangle B? Use numbers to prove your answer is correct.

_____

_____

_____

_____

_____

_____

_____

3. The formula for perimeter is $P = 2l + 2w$. If a rectangular painting has a length of 18 inches and a width of 12 inches, what is its perimeter?

   (A) 30 inches

   (B) 60 inches

   (C) 80 inches

   (D) 120 inches

Strategy

Read word problems carefully to identify the given information and what you are being asked to find.

Explain and Support Inferences
Reading: Literature

DIRECTIONS: Read the story. Then, answer the questions.

WATERLAND

"Hurray!" cried Meghan. "Today is the day we're going to Waterland!" It was a hot July day, and Meghan's mom was taking her to cool off on the water slides. Meghan's new friend, Jake, was going too. Just then, Meghan's mom came out of her bedroom. She did not look very happy. "What's the matter, Mom? Are you afraid to get wet?" Meghan teased. "I'll bet you'll melt, just like the Wicked Witch of the West!"

Mrs. Millett didn't laugh at the joke. Instead, she told the kids that she wasn't feeling well. She was too tired to drive to the water park. Meghan and Jake were disappointed. "My mom has chronic fatigue syndrome," Meghan explained. "Her illness makes her really tired. She's still a great mom."

"Thank you, dear," said Mrs. Millett. "I'm too tired to drive, but I have an idea. You can make your own Waterland, and I'll rest in the lawn chair." Meghan and Jake set up three sprinklers. They dragged the play slide to the wading pool and aimed the sprinklers on the slide. Meghan and Jake got soaking wet. Mrs. Millett sat in a lawn chair and rested. The kids played all day.

"Thank you for being so understanding," Meghan's mom said. "Now, I feel better, but I'm really hot! There's only one cure for that." She stood under the sprinkler with all her clothes on. She was drenched from head to toe. Meghan laughed and said, "Now you have chronic wet syndrome." Mrs. Millett rewarded her daughter with a big, wet hug. It turned out to be a wonderful day after all at the backyard Waterland.

Strategy As you read, pay attention to details from the story. Use the details to explain the story and to make inferences.

Test Tip Use what you already know and the details from the story to make inferences.

1. How do you think Mrs. Millett feels about not being able to take the children to Waterland?
- (A) She is glad she won't have to spend her whole day with children.
- (B) She feels sorry for herself and is glad she got out of it.
- ● She is disappointed she can't take the children.
- (D) She is hurt and confused.

Write how you know.

Possible Answer: The story says "Her illness makes her really tired".

3. How do you think Meghan feels about her mother's illness?

Possible Answer: She is disappointed when her mom can't do things, but she understands why.

2. In this story, *fatigue* means the same as ____.
- (A) to be excited
- ● to be tired
- (C) to be sad
- (D) to be sick

7

Explain and Support Inferences
Reading: Literature

DIRECTIONS: Read the story. Then, answer the questions.

THE FIRST DAY

"I don't know about this, Mom." Henry frowned. It was the first day of school, and he was walking with his mom. "Maybe I should just stay home with you and start kindergarten next year." Henry's mom laughed and fluffed his hair with her hand. They continued up the path to school.

The path was curved with lots of trees on either side. The sun came down between the branches and lit Henry's mom's face. "You're going to love school! You get to learn fun new things and make a bunch of friends," she told him.

"Sadie's older brother said the teacher was mean and the math is hard, though!" Henry was ignoring his mom's comforting words.

They continued to walk up the path until they reached a bright red door, which led to a light blue hallway. At the end of the hallway was another, smaller red door that read "Mrs. Selway's Kindergarten Room" in yellow bubble letters. Standing at the door was a short, round, older woman with silver hair.

"You must be Henry!" she said. He looked back at his mom. As she nudged him forward, Mrs. Selway opened the door, and Henry saw something he couldn't believe. Dozens of kids were playing, laughing, and having a great time! Suddenly, Henry was a little excited. After hugging his mom, he turned around and ran straight into the classroom thinking, "Maybe this won't be so bad after all."

Strategy When explaining an event or describing a character in the story, use details that are written in the story.

Test Tip Look at the characters' words and actions to determine their feelings.

1. How do you think Henry was feeling on his first day of kindergarten?
- (A) excited
- (B) sleepy
- ● nervous
- (D) sick

What details from the story support your inference?

Possible Answer: "I don't know about this, Mom." Henry frowned.

2. What does the word *comforting* mean in the story?
- (A) make something softer
- ● make someone feel better
- (C) make someone nervous
- (D) make something louder

Write how you know.

Possible Answer: Henry's mom says "comforting words" to make him feel better about school. She tells him that he will learn new things and make friends.

8

Determine Theme and Summarize Text
Reading: Literature

DIRECTIONS: Read the story. Then, answer the questions.

Maggie and Isabel went to the park on Saturday. They headed for the slides. However, they couldn't decide who should go first. Isabel said she should go first because she was older. Maggie said she should go first because Isabel was always first. Just then, their mother came over and said, "Why don't you each get on one slide and start down at the same time?" That's just what they did.

Strategy Use ideas, events, and details from a story to determine its theme.

Test Tip Find a story's theme by looking for details that tell what a major character learns during the story.

1. What is this story about?
- ● a problem that is solved
- (B) an argument at the park
- (C) sisters who get along well
- (D) brothers who lost their dog

What details helped you determine what the story is about?

Possible Answer: The sisters couldn't decide who would use the slide first. Their mom helped them solve the problem.

2. Who solves the problem in the story?
- (A) the coach
- (B) Maggie
- (C) Isabel
- ● the mother

3. What was the problem in the story?

The girls couldn't agree on who should go down the slide first.

4. What was the solution to the problem?

The girls chose different slides and went down at the same time.

5. Using details from the story, which theme best fits the story?
- (A) If you can't agree, keep talking until you do.
- (B) Always tell people how you feel.
- ● Try looking for a new solution if you can't agree.
- (D) Other people can help you solve problems.

Write how you know.

The girls kept talking about who would use the slide first. A new solution was to use two slides at the same time.

6. Write a summary of the story.

Two sisters are at a park. They both want to use the slide first. One sister feels she should go first because the other sister always goes first. They still can't decide. Then, their mother asks them to use two slides and slide down together.

9

Determine Theme and Summarize Text
Reading: Literature

DIRECTIONS: Read the story. Then, answer the questions.

Joel's hockey team had played well all season, and this was their chance to win the tournament. He was the best player.

He glanced around at his teammates. "Guys," he said, "let's skate really hard and show them how great we are!"

The team cheered and started to walk out to the ice. Joel turned around to grab his helmet, but it wasn't there. He looked under the benches and in the lockers, but his helmet wasn't anywhere. He sat down and felt his throat get tight. If he didn't have a helmet, he couldn't play.

Just then, there was a knock on the door. Joel's mom peeked her head around the locker room door. "Thank goodness," she said. "I got here just in time with your helmet."

Strategy To discover the theme, ask yourself what the overall lesson or message of the passage is.

1. What is this story about?
- ● a problem that is solved
- (B) an argument that is solved
- (C) a hockey team trying to win
- (D) hockey equipment

2. Who solves the problem in the story?
- (A) the coach
- (B) Joel
- (C) Joel's teammates
- ● the mother

3. What was the problem in the story?

Joel couldn't find his helmet before the big hockey game.

4. Which theme fits the story best?
- (A) Play hard and you will win.
- (B) Don't lose important things.
- ● People close to you will help you.
- (D) Remember that it's only a game.

Write how you know.

Joel's mom brought his helmet just in time. Joel can trust that his mom will help him solve a problem.

5. If the story on page 9 and on this page appeared together in a book of similar stories, a good title for the book would be ____.
- (A) Sports Bloopers
- ● Mom to the Rescue
- (C) Sisters Who Argue
- (D) How to Play Hockey Without a Helmet

10

Name _____ Date _____
English Language Arts

Determine the Meaning of Words and Phrases in a Text
Reading: Literature

DIRECTIONS: Read the story. Then, answer the questions.

A percussionist, someone who plays a lots of instruments, came to my school today. His name is Marco.

Marco said that by participating, or taking part, in the arts, you are helping your brain develop. This means that music, literature, and theater make you smarter! He told us about percussion and all of the different instruments he plays. One kind of instrument is a keyboard instrument, like the xylophone or marimba.

Another instrument he told us about is the timpani. Timpani are big round drums. All you need to make them change pitch is a little foot pedal, almost like a gas pedal, at the bottom of the drum.

He also told us about auxiliary instruments. Triangles, wood blocks, and maracas all are considered auxiliary, which means they are support instruments. These instruments are mostly for effect to help set a mood for different songs.

The last kind of percussion instrument Marco told us about was hand drums. Bongos and congas are both types of hand drums, along with more eccentric, or rare, drums like the cahone and djembe.

Thanks to Marco, I know a lot more about percussion and the arts than I did this morning, and I'm even thinking about trying music myself. It's cool to see how many instruments there are and how they can benefit, or help, you!

Strategy While reading, identify word clues in a story to see how ideas are related and to determine word meanings.

Test Tip The author doesn't always tell you what new words mean. You can use the context and what you already know to find the meanings.

1. Which three following instruments belong in the percussion family?
- ● drums
- ● timpani
- Ⓒ guitar
- ● triangle

2. What are auxiliary instruments?

Possible Answer: Auxiliary instruments are support instruments used for effect.

3. If you *participate* in an activity, what are you doing?
- Ⓐ quitting the activity
- ● taking part in the activity
- Ⓒ watching an activity
- Ⓓ referring to an activity

Which words in the story helped you with your answer?

taking part

4. What is a synonym for *eccentric*?

rare

11

Name _____ Date _____
English Language Arts

Determine the Meaning of Words and Phrases in a Text
Reading: Literature

DIRECTIONS: Read the story. Then, answer the questions.

"Daddy, Daddy!" Sarah shouted, as she entered the kitchen carefully carrying the fragile glass jar in her hands. It was dusk, and the sun was almost completely set. Sarah's dad turned from the sink to greet her, only to find a large glass jar of fireflies thrust into his face. "Look, look!"

Calmly, Sarah's dad examined the jar of illuminating bugs. "Isn't it cool how they light up like that?" Sarah exclaimed. "It is!" her father replied. "Every time they light up like that, they are actually taking a big gulp of oxygen, or air. It's how they breathe! When the light goes out, they're all out of breath."

"If they can't breathe anymore, they will die. But, we can help them live longer if we keep them out of the jar and in the backyard. There's more oxygen out there than there is in that jar," her dad said, smiling.

Shocked, Sarah immediately ran outside, only to return with a sad face and an empty jar. She began to cry, so her dad asked what was wrong. "I miss them!" Sarah exclaimed.

Taking Sarah's hand, her dad led her outside to the moon rising and the fireflies floating in and out of sight. "We can still see them, silly! We can even see more of them. Don't cry. You're helping them live longer, happier lives."

Maybe Sarah's dad was right. They looked a lot prettier floating around in the grass than a jar, anyway.

Strategy Try replacing an unknown word with different meanings to see if that meaning makes sense in the sentence.

1. What does the word *illuminating* mean?
- Ⓐ flying
- ● shining
- Ⓒ sleeping
- Ⓓ eating

Write how you know.

Possible Answer: The words near the word *illuminating* are *light up*. Some objects that shine have light.

2. Why do fireflies need oxygen?

It is in the air they breathe to stay alive.

3. What time of day is *dusk*?
- Ⓐ early morning
- Ⓑ mid-afternoon
- ● early evening
- Ⓓ late night

Which words from the story helped you answer?

Possible Answer: "the sun was almost completely set"

4. How did Sarah's father convince Sarah to let the fireflies out of the jar?

Possible Answer: He explained why the fireflies needed to be outside.

12

Name _____ Date _____
English Language Arts

Describe Characters, Settings, and Events
Reading: Literature

DIRECTIONS: Read the story. Then, answer the questions.

THE FOX AND THE GRAPES

One warm summer day, a fox was walking along when he noticed a bunch of grapes on a vine above him. Cool, juicy grapes would taste so good. The more he thought about it, the more the fox wanted those grapes. He tried standing on his tiptoes. When he jumped high in the air, he tried getting a running start before he jumped. But, no matter what he tried, the fox could not reach the grapes. As he angrily walked away, the fox muttered, "They were probably sour, anyway!"

MORAL: A person (or fox) sometimes pretends he or she does not want something he or she cannot have.

Strategy As you read, pick out specific details from the story to describe the setting, characters, and events.

Test Tip Use a character's words and actions to understand the reasons behind them.

1. Describe the setting of the fable.

Possible Answer: It is a warm summer day. The fable takes place outdoors.

2. Why did the fox want the grapes so badly?
- ● He was warm and thirsty.
- Ⓑ He was hungry.
- Ⓒ He didn't want anyone else to get them.
- Ⓓ He wanted to make grape jelly.

3. The fox was very determined to get the grapes. What details in the story help you understand what the word *determined* means?

Possible Answer: "He tried standing on his tiptoes. He tried jumping high in the air. He tried getting a running start before he jumped."

Test Tip
A moral is a lesson that fables teach on how you should or should not act.

4. What detail supports the moral, "A person (or fox) sometimes pretends that he or she does not want something he or she cannot have."
- Ⓐ "The more he thought about it, the more the fox wanted those grapes."
- Ⓑ "He tried standing on his tiptoes."
- Ⓒ "But, no matter what he tried, the fox could not reach the grapes."
- ● "As he angrily walked away, the fox muttered, 'They were probably sour anyway!'"

5. Describe the character of fox using details from the story.

Possible Answer: Fox tries very hard to get what he wants. The story says he tries running, jumping, and reaching for the grapes. He also gets angry when he can't reach the grapes. He is not very patient.

13

Name _____ Date _____
English Language Arts

Describe Characters, Settings, and Events
Reading: Literature

DIRECTIONS: Read the story. Then, answer the questions.

It was Friday, and school had just ended. Maria stepped off the bus and began to walk home. As she approached her front yard, she noticed something different. There was barking coming from the backyard. "What could that be?" thought Maria. "We don't have a dog."

However, when she walked into her backyard, she found just that. A dog! "Woof, woof, woof!" it greeted her with its tail wagging. "Surprise!" Maria's parents yelled. "We got you a puppy. His name is Spot." Maria let out a squeak in surprise and jumped into the air. "I can't believe it!" she shouted.

Maria and Spot began to run to each other until he jumped up and rolled onto the ground. Maria giggled, and Spot licked her face. "Do you want to take him for a walk?" Maria's father asked. Maria nodded her head with a big grin on her face.

Her dad showed her how to put on Spot's leash, and they all went to the front yard to walk Spot. He pulled and tugged, but after a while, he began to walk with Maria. It made her happy. While they walked, Maria's dad told her about all of the responsibilities of owning a dog. "I promise to take care of him," she said.

When they got home, Maria sat in the backyard with Spot and fed him dog treats. He wagged his tail and licked his lips. Then, he flopped over so Maria could rub his belly. Maria patted him gently, smiling the whole time. Over and over, she told herself how happy she was.

When her dad called her to come in for bed, Maria got up and Spot followed. Before they got inside, she whispered, "I love you, Spot." Spot let out a soft "woof," and they walked in together.

Strategy As you read, ask yourself Who? What? Where? When? How? and Why? Use the answers to find details about characters, settings, and events.

Test Tip The setting of a story is not only where the story happens, but also when it happens.

1. Describe the setting of this story. Use details from the story.

The story takes place on a Friday afternoon and evening at Maria's house and in her yard.

2. Do you think Maria is a responsible girl? Explain your answer.

Possible Answer: Yes, Maria is responsible because her parents thought she could take care of a puppy.

3. How does Maria feel about getting a new puppy?
- Ⓐ upset
- Ⓑ overwhelmed
- Ⓒ scared
- ● excited

Write how you know.

Possible Answer: Maria squeaks and tells her parents she can't believe it. She grins and walks Spot right away.

14

Explain Differences Between
Poetry, Drama, and Prose
Reading: Literature

DIRECTIONS: Read the poem. Then, answer the questions.

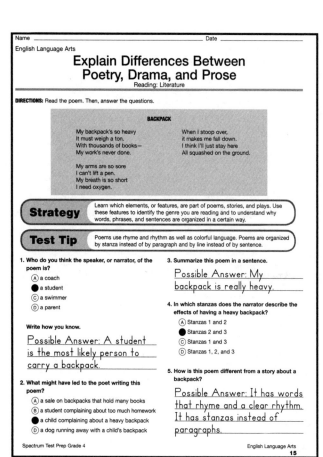

BACKPACK

My backpack's so heavy
It must weigh a ton.
With thousands of books—
My work's never done.

My arms are so sore
I can't lift a pen.
My breath is so short
I need oxygen.

When I stoop over,
it makes me fall down.
I think I'll just stay here
All squashed on the ground.

Strategy Learn which elements, or features, are part of poems, stories, and plays. Use these features to identify the genre you are reading and to understand why words, phrases, and sentences are organized in a certain way.

Test Tip Poems use rhyme and rhythm as well as colorful language. Poems are organized by stanza instead of by paragraph and by line instead of by sentence.

1. Who do you think the speaker, or narrator, of the poem is?
   - Ⓐ a coach
   - ● a student
   - Ⓒ a swimmer
   - Ⓓ a parent

Write how you know.

Possible Answer: A student is the most likely person to carry a backpack.

2. What might have led to the poet writing this poem?
   - Ⓐ a sale on backpacks that hold many books
   - Ⓑ a student complaining about too much homework
   - ● a child complaining about a heavy backpack
   - Ⓓ a dog running away with a child's backpack

3. Summarize this poem in a sentence.

Possible Answer: My backpack is really heavy.

4. In which stanzas does the narrator describe the effects of having a heavy backpack?
   - Ⓐ Stanzas 1 and 2
   - ● Stanzas 2 and 3
   - Ⓒ Stanzas 1 and 3
   - Ⓓ Stanzas 1, 2, and 3

5. How is this poem different from a story about a backpack?

Possible Answer: It has words that rhyme and a clear rhythm. It has stanzas instead of paragraphs.

Explain Differences Between
Poetry, Drama, and Prose
Reading: Literature

DIRECTIONS: Read the poem. Then, answer the questions.

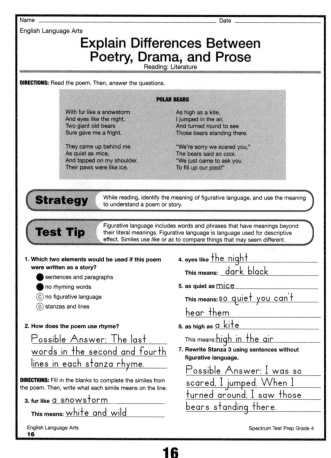

POLAR BEARS

With fur like a snowstorm
And eyes like the night,
Two giant old bears
Sure gave me a fright.

They came up behind me
As quiet as mice,
And tapped on my shoulder.
Their paws were like ice.

As high as a kite,
I jumped in the air,
And turned round to see
Those bears standing there.

"We're sorry we scared you,"
The bears said so cool.
"We just came to ask you
To fill up our pool!"

Strategy While reading, identify the meaning of figurative language, and use the meaning to understand a poem or story.

Test Tip Figurative language includes words and phrases that have meanings beyond their literal meanings. Figurative language is language used for descriptive effect. Similes use *like* or *as* to compare things that may seem different.

1. Which two elements would be used if this poem were written as a story?
   - ● sentences and paragraphs
   - ● no rhyming words
   - Ⓒ no figurative language
   - Ⓓ stanzas and lines

2. How does the poem use rhyme?

Possible Answer: The last words in the second and fourth lines in each stanza rhyme.

DIRECTIONS: Fill in the blanks to complete the similes from the poem. Then, write what each simile means on the line.

3. fur like a snowstorm
   This means: white and wild

4. eyes like the night
   This means: dark black

5. as quiet as mice
   This means: so quiet you can't hear them

6. as high as a kite
   This means: high in the air

7. Rewrite Stanza 3 using sentences without figurative language.

Possible Answer: I was so scared, I jumped. When I turned around, I saw those bears standing there.

Explain Differences Between
Poetry, Drama, and Prose
Reading: Literature

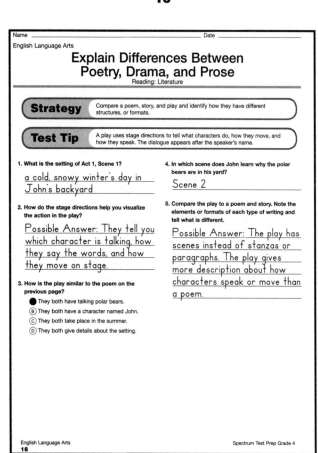

Strategy Compare a poem, story, and play and identify how they have different structures, or formats.

Test Tip A play uses stage directions to tell what characters do, how they move, and how they speak. The dialogue appears after the speaker's name.

1. What is the setting of Act 1, Scene 1?

a cold, snowy winter's day in John's backyard

2. How do the stage directions help you visualize the action in the play?

Possible Answer: They tell you which character is talking, how they say the words, and how they move on stage.

3. How is the play similar to the poem on the previous page?
   - ● They both have talking polar bears.
   - Ⓑ They both have a character named John.
   - Ⓒ They both take place in the summer.
   - Ⓓ They both give details about the setting.

4. In which scene does John learn why the polar bears are in his yard?

Scene 2

5. Compare the play to a poem and story. Note the elements or formats of each type of writing and tell what is different.

Possible Answer: The play has scenes instead of stanzas or paragraphs. The play gives more description about how characters speak or move than a poem.

Compare and Contrast Different Points of View
Reading: Literature

DIRECTIONS: Use the stories to answer the questions.

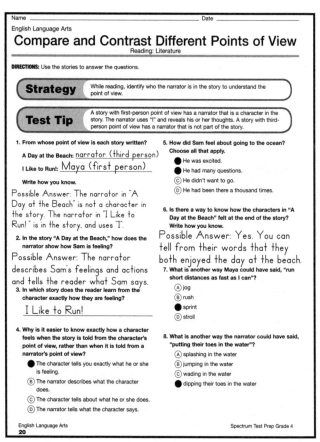

Strategy While reading, identify who the narrator is in the story to understand the point of view.

Test Tip A story with first-person point of view has a narrator that is a character in the story. The narrator uses "I" and reveals his or her thoughts. A story with third-person point of view has a narrator that is not part of the story.

1. From whose point of view is each story written?
   A Day at the Beach: narrator (third person)
   I Like to Run!: Maya (first person)

Write how you know.

Possible Answer: The narrator in "A Day at the Beach" is not a character in the story. The narrator in "I Like to Run!" is in the story, and uses "I".

2. In the story "A Day at the Beach," how does the narrator show how Sam is feeling?

Possible Answer: The narrator describes Sam's feelings and actions and tells what Sam says.

3. In which story does the reader learn from the character exactly how they are feeling?

I Like to Run!

4. Why is it easier to know exactly how a character feels when the story is told from the character's point of view, rather than when it is told from a narrator's point of view?
   - ● The character tells you exactly what he or she is feeling.
   - Ⓑ The narrator describes what the character does.
   - Ⓒ The character tells about what he or she does.
   - Ⓓ The narrator tells what the character says.

5. How did Sam feel about going to the ocean? Choose all that apply.
   - ● He was excited.
   - ● He had many questions.
   - Ⓒ He didn't want to go.
   - Ⓓ He had been there a thousand times.

6. Is there a way to know how the characters in "A Day at the Beach" felt at the end of the story? Write how you know.

Possible Answer: Yes. You can tell from their words that they both enjoyed the day at the beach.

7. What is another way Maya could have said, "run short distances as fast as I can"?
   - Ⓐ jog
   - Ⓑ rush
   - ● sprint
   - Ⓓ stroll

8. What is another way the narrator could have said, "putting their toes in the water"?
   - Ⓐ splashing in the water
   - Ⓑ jumping in the water
   - Ⓒ wading in the water
   - ● dipping their toes in the water

Determine the Meaning of Words and Phrases
Language

DIRECTIONS: Read the passage. Then, answer the questions.

Ancient myths often depict monsters with multiple heads. But, that may not be so far from reality. A 2-headed snake is rare, but they do exist.

A 2-headed snake was discovered in Spain. This snake is not poisonous. It was a 2-month-old ladder snake that was about 8 inches long. The snake was lucky to be captured, since it would not have had much chance of surviving in the wild.

The snake takes a long time to eat, making it vulnerable to predators. While feeding, the 2 heads fight over which will swallow the food. Additionally, because snakes use their sense of smell to find food, if one head smells prey on the other head, it will attack it.

The heads also have a hard time deciding which direction to go. If it were attacked, it would have a hard time escaping.

Two-headed snakes do not seem to be a product of evolution. Much like conjoined twins, it appears that the embryo, or egg, starts to split into 2 but does not complete the division.

Although 2-headed snakes can survive in captivity, their chances of surviving in the wild are almost zero.

Strategy Determine the meaning of unknown words by identifying synonyms and antonyms.

Test Tip Make sure you read all of the answer choices. When you think you see the correct answer, place your finger next to it.

1. Which word is a synonym for *vulnerable*?
- (A) safe
- ● helpless
- (C) dangerous
- (D) scary

Write how you know.

Possible Answer: None of the other answers sound right in the sentence. The snake is busy eating. It is helpless against predators.

2. What is prey?

food

3. What do you think *conjoined* means?
- (A) separate
- (B) identical
- (C) fraternal
- ● attached

Which words in the passage helped you choose the meaning?

Possible Answer: multiple head, 2-headed, division

4. What is an *embryo*?

an egg

Demonstrate Understanding of Figurative Language, Word Relationships, and Nuances
Language

DIRECTIONS: Choose or write a synonym of the underlined word.

Strategy Read sentences carefully to make sure you understand the meaning that makes sense within the sentence.

Test Tip Look for words and phrases that do not have literal meanings.

1. The boy scaled the <u>high</u> fence.

Possible Answer: tall

2. Please <u>paste</u> the paper to your stick.

Possible Answer: glue

3. The rabbit ran <u>swiftly</u> through the grass.
- (A) slowly
- (B) smoothly
- ● quickly
- (D) on the land

4. Gazelles and impalas are <u>prey</u> to the cheetah.
- ● food
- (B) friends
- (C) similar
- (D) predators

DIRECTIONS: Choose the meaning for each simile or metaphor.

Test Tip

Remember that metaphors and similes compare seemingly different things to show how they are alike. Metaphors do not use the words *like* or *as*.

5. The papers fluttered like the wings of a butterfly.
- ● moved in the breeze
- (B) sat on the table
- (C) fell on the floor
- (D) slipped from my hand

6. The stars are diamonds in the night.
- (A) Stars are valuable at night.
- (B) Stars can be made into jewelry.
- ● Stars shine brightly in the night sky.
- (D) Stars are shaped like diamonds.

DIRECTIONS: Choose or write an antonym of the underlined word.

7. <u>valuable</u> painting
- (A) strange
- ● expensive
- ● worthless
- (D) humorous

8. <u>loose</u> tie

Possible Answer: tight

9. <u>narrow</u> ledge

Possible Answer: wide

Demonstrate Understanding of Figurative Language, Word Relationships, and Nuances
Language

Strategy Compare the literal and nonliteral meanings of words and phrases to find the right meaning.

DIRECTIONS: Read the passage. Then, match the phrases in Column A with their meanings in Column B.

You may have heard people use certain words or phrases that have a particular meaning in the area or culture in which you live. Someone who is not from your area or culture may not understand what those words or phrases mean. These phrases or sayings are called *colloquialisms*. Many cultures develop their own colloquialisms.

Here is an example of one that is used in the United States:

"Hold your horses" means to *be patient* or *slow down*.

Test Tip Read all the choices before you mark your answer.

	Column A		Column B
f	1. bury the hatchet	a.	to do something difficult
a	2. bite the bullet	b.	to die
c	3. forty winks	c.	to take a nap
h	4. knee high to a grasshopper	d.	to do something immediately
g	5. squirrel away	e.	to be very tired
d	6. strike while the iron is hot	f.	to make peace with someone
e	7. worn to a frazzle	g.	to store up for future use
b	8. kick the bucket	h.	to be very short

DIRECTIONS: Below are examples of figurative language used in Australia. Try to match the phrases in Column A with their meanings in Column B.

	Column A		Column B
b	9. ankle biter	a.	to be in a rage
d	10. it's gone walkabout	b.	a small child
a	11. mad as a cut snake	c.	to be stranded
c	12. up a gum tree	d.	to have lost something

Write an Opinion Piece
Writing

DIRECTIONS: An opinion paragraph tells how you think or feel about a topic. It gives reasons why you think or feel that way. Write an opinion paragraph for your parents on where to go on a vacation. Your paragraph should have the following:

- A sentence to introduce your topic
- A statement of your opinion
- An organizational structure
- Reasons to support your opinion
- Facts and details to support your reasons
- Linking words and phrases to connect your opinion and reasons
- A sentence to end your paragraph

Strategy Plan your writing by stating your opinion and listing reasons you have that opinion. Then, begin writing. When you are finished writing, read your paragraph to yourself. Make sure you included everything listed in the directions. Make sure your writing is clear and fix any errors.

Test Tip An opinion must be supported with reasons. Reasons tell why you think or feel a certain way. Include details that support your reasons.

I want to go to:
Reason 1:
Details:
Reason 2:
Details:
Reason 3:
Details:
Conclusion:

Plans will vary.

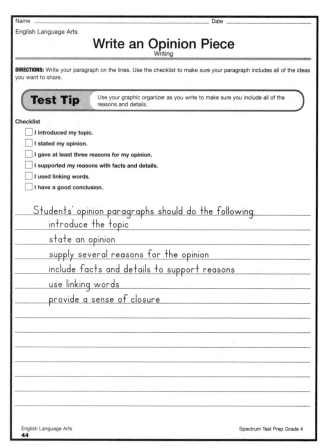

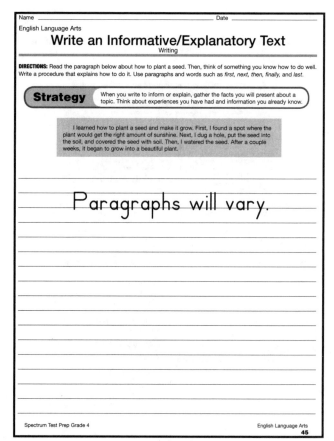

Page 48

Write an Informative/Explanatory Text
Writing

DIRECTIONS: Write your paragraph on the lines. Use the checklist to make sure your paragraph is organized clearly and includes all of the information.

Test Tip Use your outline as you write your informational passage to present your ideas and facts clearly.

Checklist
☐ I introduced my topic.
☐ I gave at least three facts about my topic.
☐ I supported my facts with details.
☐ I grouped information together.
☐ I used specific words.
☐ I have a good conclusion.

Student should do the following:
introduce the topic
state facts about the topic
group similar facts together within paragraphs
supply specific details to support the facts
provide a sense of closure

48

Page 49

Write a Narrative
Writing

DIRECTIONS: A narrative is a story that tells about real or imagined events. Write a narrative about a problem you had and how you solved it. Your paragraph should have the following:

- A narrator and/or characters
- A natural sequence of events
- Dialogue
- Descriptions of actions, thoughts, and feelings
- Time words and phrases to show the order of events
- Concrete words and sensory details
- A sentence to end your paragraph

Strategy Plan a narrative by choosing people, places, and events that will be in the story. Remember that a story should have a beginning, middle, and end.

Test Tip Include details that help your readers understand the event and imagine it in their minds.

Situation or Problem:

Event 1:

Paragraphs will vary.

Details:

Event 2:

Details:

Event 3:

Details:

Conclusion:

49

Page 50

Write a Narrative
Writing

DIRECTIONS: Write your paragraph on the lines. Use the checklist to make sure your paragraph is organized clearly and includes all of the information.

Test Tip Use your organizer as you write your narrative to make sure events are in order and that you use details.

Checklist
☐ I introduced my narrator and/or characters.
☐ I told what the problem in the story was.
☐ I wrote a clear sequence of events that happened.
☐ I used dialogue and wrote about the characters' thoughts, actions, and feelings.
☐ I used time words.
☐ I used concrete words and sensory details.
☐ I have a good conclusion.

Student should do the following:
include a narrator and/or characters
follow a natural sequence of events
include dialogue
include descriptions of characters' actions, thoughts, and feelings
use time words and phrases to show the order of events
use concrete words and sensory details
write a satisfying conclusion

50

Page 51

Understand Editing and Revising
Writing

DIRECTIONS: Choose or write the best answer.

Strategy Revise to make sure your writing makes sense. Then, edit to fix errors. Use what you know about nouns, verbs, adjectives, and adverbs to make correct choices when you edit.

Test Tip When you are revising a paragraph, read it out loud to yourself. Listen for anything that does not sound right or does not make sense.

1. Rewrite the following fragments as complete sentences. **Possible Answers:**
playing outside
The dogs are playing outside.
a few people in this class
A few people in this class forgot their pencils today.
on the roof
I hear birds on the roof.
in the air
The kite flew high in the air.

2. Explain why it is important to use complete sentences in writing.
Possible Answer: A sentence fragment is an incomplete idea. It is missing a subject or a verb. Complete sentences show complete ideas.

3. Find the word that is spelled correctly and that best fits the sentence.
Please _____ your work before turning it in.
(A) revew
(B) reeview
● review
(D) reveiw

He is my best _____.
(A) frind
(B) frend
● friend
(D) freind

We _____ her to arrive at noon.
(A) acept
(B) espect
(C) accept
● expect

4. Rewrite the sentences using correct capitalization and punctuation.
tyson began singing the star-spangled banner
Tyson began singing "The Star-Spangled Banner."

I'm really glad you are here abby said
"I'm really glad you are here," Abby said.

5. Combine the two simple sentences into a compound sentence.
Sasha flew to Chicago. She took a train to Milwaukee.
Sasha flew to Chicago and then took a train to Milwaukee.

51

Understand Editing and Revising
Writing

DIRECTIONS: Choose or write the best answer.

Strategy Reread your writing out loud to find punctuation mistakes. To find spelling and capitalization errors, try reading backward, looking at each word.

1. Use each word or phrase in a sentence.

whom   Possible Answers:

To whom should I give the book?

_____

where

Where are we going for dinner?

_____

will be going

We will be going to the zoo

tomorrow.

_____

must

I must take my medicine

every day.

2. Which sentences are written correctly? Choose all that apply.

(A) We went to there house.
● I gave them their gifts.
● Two of the birds flew away.
(D) I was to late to see the movie.

3. Revise the story so it sounds better. Choose words and phrases that precisely show ideas and punctuation for effect.

I saw this thing on the street. It was a red, big bag. I wondered what was in it. I looked inside. It was something round and small. It was something shiny. I had found a gold coin.

Possible Answer: I saw
something lying on the street.
It was a big, red bag. I
wondered what was in it. I
peeked inside and saw
something small and round. It
was very shiny. I had found a
gold coin!

_____

_____

52

Strategy Review

In this section, you will review the strategies you learned and apply them to practice the skills.

Strategy Use details from the story to make inferences, understand theme, and determine meaning.

EXAMPLE
Read the story carefully. Then, answer the questions using details from the story.

A BUMPY RIDE
When we first climbed into the car and strapped on our safety belts, I wasn't very nervous. I was sitting right next to my big brother, and he had done this many times before. As we started to climb the hill, however, I could feel my heart jump into my throat.
"Brian?" I asked nervously. "Is this supposed to be so noisy?"
"Sure, Matthew," Brian answered. "It always does that."
A minute later, we were going so fast down the hill, I didn't have time to think. With a twist, a loop, and a bunch of fast turns, everyone on board screamed in delight. No wonder this was one of the most popular rides in the park. By the time the car pulled into the station and we got off the ride, I was ready to do it again!

How does the description of the scene help you know the setting of the story?
The story describes a car with a safety belt climbing a hill and then going fast down a hill, around turns, and through twists and loops. This tells you that the setting is an amusement park and the boys are on a roller coaster.

1. How did the character's feelings change throughout the story?

Possible Answer: When he got
on the ride, he wasn't nervous.
Once the ride started, he
started feeling a little nervous.
When the ride was over, he
was excited to do it again.

2. How do you think Matthew will feel the next time he gets on a roller coaster?

He will be excited to ride.

3. How did the strategy help you answer these questions?

Possible Answer: Looking at
the details of the story
allowed me to make
connections to what I know
about amusement parks.

53

Strategy Review

DIRECTIONS: Read the story carefully. Then, answer the questions.

Strategy Look carefully at visuals such as illustrations, diagrams, or graphs to see how they connect to the story.

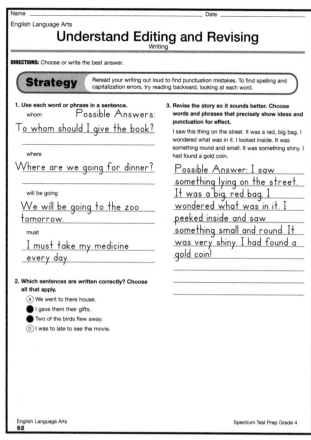

Most Popular Sports at Lake Bluff Elementary School

Describe what this graph is about.
To understand a visual within a passage, look at the words around and on the visual. This is a bar graph. Notice sports along the bottom and numbers along the side. The title tells you this graph is about popular sports at an elementary school.

1. What is the most popular sport at Lake Bluff Elementary School?
● soccer
(B) football
(C) gymnastics
(D) ice skating

2. In what type of passage would you expect to see a graph like this?

a nonfiction passage about
sports at elementary schools

Strategy
Reread stories to make comparisons, draw conclusions, or support inferences.

THE UN-BIRTHDAY
In my family, we don't celebrate birthdays—at least not like most families. My friends say I have an "un-birthday." The tradition started with my grandmother. She and my grandfather grew up in Poland. They escaped before World War II and made their way to America. When they arrived, they were so grateful, they decided to share what they had with others. On their birthdays, they gave each other just one small gift. Then, they each bought a gift for someone who needed it more than they did.

As you read, think about how the story compares to what you know and how you celebrate birthdays in your family.

3. How would you describe an un-birthday to someone?

Possible Answer: An un-birthday
is when you use your birthday as
an excuse to share with those
less fortunate than you.

4. Why did the narrator's grandparents decide to celebrate an un-birthday?

They felt fortunate to escape
from Poland before World War
II, so they wanted to share their
happiness with others.

54

Strategy Review

Strategy Identify a story's structure, see how ideas are related, and clarify word meanings by using word clues.

Ethan and Austin have two dogs. Both dogs are about the same age. Sam is 6 years old, and Xavier is 7 years old.
Sam is a Collie-Shepherd mix. He is black with a white chest. Sam weighs 75 pounds. In the winter, Sam's fur grows very long. He looks like a shaggy black bear. Sam has a straight tail with lots of fur hanging off of it.
Xavier is a Chow-Labrador mix. He is tan. His fur is very short, and his tail curls up toward his back. Xavier also weighs about 75 pounds.
Both dogs are very sweet. They let the boys use them as pillows. They like to run and play in the backyard. Sam likes to chase balls and bring them back to be thrown again. But, Xavier just likes to eat them.

When you read the story, words like *both* and *also* tell you the dogs are being compared. Words like *but* tell you the dogs are being contrasted.

1. How are Sam and Xavier alike?
Possible Answers: They are
about the same age; they are
about the same weight; they are
both sweet.

2. How are Sam and Xavier different?
Possible Answers: Sam is black, and
Xavier is tan; Sam likes to play fetch,
but Xavier likes to eat the ball.

Strategy
Use an outline to plan your writing.

Before you start writing, make a plan of what you are going to include. Use an outline or other graphic organizer to keep your ideas in order.

EXAMPLE
Write a report about horses.
I. Breeds
   A. Abaco Barb
   B. American Paint Horse
   C. Andalusia
II. Appearances
   A. Hair
   B. Mane
   C. Tail
III. Interesting Facts
   A. Where are they from?
   B. How are they used?
   C. Horse History

3. Use an outline to plan a report about an animal.
I.   Students should provide
   A. information for a paragraph
   B. about a specific animal.
   C. _____
II. _____
   A. _____
   B. _____
   C. _____
III. _____
   A. _____
   B. _____
   C. _____

55

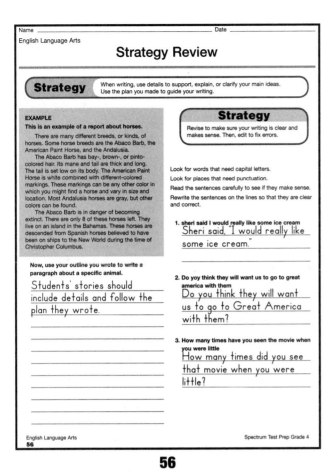

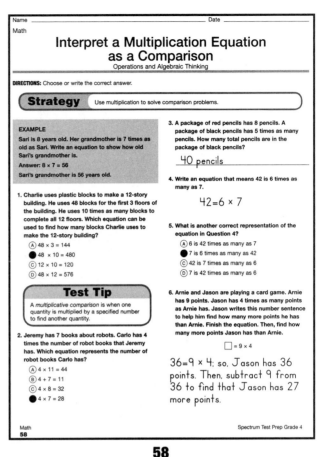

Page 56 — English Language Arts — Strategy Review

Strategy: When writing, use details to support, explain, or clarify your main ideas. Use the plan you made to guide your writing.

EXAMPLE
This is an example of a report about horses.

There are many different breeds, or kinds, of horses. Some horse breeds are the Abaco Barb, the American Paint Horse, and the Andalusia.

The Abaco Barb has bay-, brown-, or pinto-colored hair. Its mane and tail are thick and long. The tail is set low on its body. The American Paint Horse is white combined with different-colored markings. These markings can be any other color in which you might find a horse and vary in size and location. Most Andalusia horses are gray, but other colors can be found.

The Abaco Barb is in danger of becoming extinct. There are only 8 of these horses left. They live on an island in the Bahamas. These horses are descended from Spanish horses believed to have been on ships to the New World during the time of Christopher Columbus.

Now, use your outline you wrote to write a paragraph about a specific animal.

Students' stories should include details and follow the plan they wrote.

Strategy: Revise to make sure your writing is clear and makes sense. Then, edit to fix errors.

Look for words that need capital letters.
Look for places that need punctuation.
Read the sentences carefully to see if they make sense.
Rewrite the sentences on the lines so that they are clear and correct.

1. sheri said I would really like some ice cream
Sheri said, "I would really like some ice cream."

2. Do yoy think they will want us to go to great america with them
Do you think they will want us to go to Great America with them?

3. How many times have you seen the movie when you were little
How many times did you see that movie when you were little?

English Language Arts
56
Spectrum Test Prep Grade 4

56

Page 58 — Math — Interpret a Multiplication Equation as a Comparison
Operations and Algebraic Thinking

DIRECTIONS: Choose or write the correct answer.

Strategy: Use multiplication to solve comparison problems.

EXAMPLE
Sari is 8 years old. Her grandmother is 7 times as old as Sari. Write an equation to show how old Sari's grandmother is.
Answer: $8 \times 7 = 56$
Sari's grandmother is 56 years old.

1. Charlie uses plastic blocks to make a 12-story building. He uses 48 blocks for the first 3 floors of the building. He uses 10 times as many blocks to complete all 12 floors. Which equation can be used to find how many blocks Charlie uses to make the 12-story building?
   A $48 \times 3 = 144$
   ● $48 \times 10 = 480$
   C $12 \times 10 = 120$
   D $48 \times 12 = 576$

Test Tip
A *multiplicative comparison* is when one quantity is multiplied by a specified number to find another quantity.

2. Jeremy has 7 books about robots. Carlo has 4 times the number of robot books that Jeremy has. Which equation represents the number of robot books Carlo has?
   A $4 \times 11 = 44$
   B $4 + 7 = 11$
   C $4 \times 8 = 32$
   ● $4 \times 7 = 28$

3. A package of red pencils has 8 pencils. A package of black pencils has 5 times as many pencils. How many total pencils are in the package of black pencils?
   40 pencils

4. Write an equation that means 42 is 6 times as many as 7.
   $42 = 6 \times 7$

5. What is another correct representation of the equation in Question 4?
   A 6 is 42 times as many as 7
   ● 7 is 6 times as many as 42
   C 42 is 7 times as many as 6
   D 7 is 42 times as many as 6

6. Arnie and Jason are playing a card game. Arnie has 9 points. Jason has 4 times as many points as Arnie has. Jason writes this number sentence to help him find how many more points he has than Arnie. Finish the equation. Then, find how many more points Jason has than Arnie.
   $\square = 9 \times 4$
   $36 = 9 \times 4$; so, Jason has 36 points. Then, subtract 9 from 36 to find that Jason has 27 more points.

Math
58
Spectrum Test Prep Grade 4

58

Page 59 — Math — Solve Multiplicative Comparison Problems: Multiply and Divide
Operations and Algebraic Thinking

DIRECTIONS: Choose or write the correct answer.

Strategy: Use multiplication and division to solve multiplicative comparison problems.

EXAMPLE
A music CD costs $9 on sale. A movie DVD on sale costs 3 times as much. How much does the movie DVD cost?
Write an equation and solve it. Let c represent the cost of the DVD.
$c = 9 \times 3$
$c = 27$
The movie DVD costs $27.

Test Tip
This is one kind of *multiplicative comparison* problem where you are finding an unknown product.

3. There are 9 boys in the cafeteria line. There are 2 times as many girls in the cafeteria line. Write a number sentence that can be used to find g, the number of girls in the line. Then, solve the number sentence.
   $9 \times 2 = g$. $g = 18$ girls

4. A cook is making pasta sauce. She has 64 tomatoes. She also has green peppers. The number of tomatoes is 8 times the number of peppers. Write a division equation and multiplication equation that can be used to find the number of peppers, p, the cook has. Solve the equation.
   $64 \div 8 = p$ and $8 \times p = 64$; there are 8 peppers.

1. Andrea built a small puzzle with 72 pieces. This is 3 times as many pieces as in Kyle's puzzle. Which equation can be used to find how many pieces, p, are in Kyle's puzzle?
   ● $72 \div 3 = p$
   B $72 \times 3 = p$
   C $72 + 3 = p$
   D $72 - 3 = p$

2. A flea can jump 130 times its own height. If you could do the same, and your height is 54 inches, which equation could you solve to find how high, h, you could jump?
   A $h = 130 + 54$
   ● $h = 130 \times 54$
   C $54 = h \times 130$
   D $130 = 54 \times h$

Spectrum Test Prep Grade 4
Math
59

59

Page 60 — Math — Solve Multiplicative Comparison Problems: Multiply and Divide
Operations and Algebraic Thinking

DIRECTIONS: Choose or write the correct answer.

5. Rianna has 24 stickers. This is 4 times the number of stickers that Alonzo has. Which of these show how to find how many stickers, s, Alonzo has? Choose all that apply.
   ● (dots)
   (dots) Number of stickers Alonzo has
   $4 \times s = 24$
   C (dots) Number of stickers Alonzo has
   D $24 + 24 + 24 + 24 = s$

Test Tip
Making a drawing can help you visualize a problem.

6. Michiko loves flowers. She has 4 huge sunflowers in her garden and 5 times as many red rose bushes as sunflowers. She has 2 times as many yellow rose bushes as red ones. How many yellow rose bushes are in Michiko's garden? Show your work.
   40 yellow rose bushes;
   $4 \times 5 \times 2 = 40$

7. Diane's grandfather is 63 years old. The equation shows he is 7 times as old as Diane. How many years old is Diane? Show how you know.
   $63 = 7 \times \square$
   9 years old. Divide 63 by 7 to get 9.

8. Sylvia and Marta are each making a paper link chain to decorate for the class party. Sylvia's chain is 28 inches long. This is 4 times the length of Marta's chain, m. Which equation can be used to find out how long Marta's chain is? Choose all that apply.
   A $28 \times 4 = m$
   B $m \times 28 = 4$
   ● $28 \div 4 = m$
   ● $m \times 4 = 28$

Math
60
Spectrum Test Prep Grade 4

60

Solve Multi-Step Problems: Add, Subtract, Multiply, and Divide
Operations and Algebraic Thinking

DIRECTIONS: Choose or write the correct answer.

Strategy — Use the order of operations as you solve problems.

EXAMPLE
Sarah, Dora, and Ruby had $45 to spend at the mall. They spent $15 on food and evenly split the rest. How much did each girl get? Show how you got your answer.

This is a multi-step problem. Write an equation and solve it. Let *m* represent how much money each girl gets.

m = (45 - 15) ÷ 3
m = 30 ÷ 3
m = 10
Each girl gets $10.

$n = (36+67+53) ÷4;$
$n = 156 ÷ 4; n = 39$ toys

1. Simon is helping his younger brother build a tower with 88 blocks. For the bottom layer, Simon makes 5 rows with 4 blocks in each row. How many blocks are left to build the rest of the tower?
   - (A) 81 blocks
   - (B) 79 blocks
   - (C) 83 blocks
   - ● 68 blocks

2. For three days, Jon and his friends collected toys for their school's annual toy drive. Their work is shown in the table below. They will give the same number of toys to 4 different childcare centers. Write and solve an equation to find the number of toys, *n*, that each center will get.

Day	Number of Toys
Monday	36
Tuesday	67
Wednesday	53

3. Mr. Gomez owns a sports store. He orders 24 caps from Company A and 35 caps from Company B. When they arrive, he places them on shelves that hold 9 caps each. How many shelves will Mr. Gomez need to hold all the caps? Show your work.

7 shelves;
24 + 35 = 59;
59 ÷ 9 = 6 r5

Test Tip
Remember the order of operations when you solve multi-step problems. Do operations inside parentheses first, and multiply and divide before you add and subtract.

4. Sari and her family drove 9½ hours to the beach. On the first day, they drove 289 miles. On the second day, they drove 377 miles. If they drove at a steady rate each day with no stops, which is the best estimate of how many miles per hour they drove?
   - ● 70 miles per hour
   - (B) 50 miles per hour
   - (C) 60 miles per hour
   - (D) 74 miles per hour

5. Explain how you got your answer in Question 4.
   Possible Answer: Round each distance up and add 400 + 300 = 700. Then, round 9½ to 10 and divide the sum mentally: 700 ÷ 10 = 70.

61

Solve Multi-Step Problems: Add, Subtract, Multiply, and Divide
Operations and Algebraic Thinking

DIRECTIONS: Choose or write the correct answer.

Strategy — Use basic operations rules. For multi-step problems, complete operations from left to right.

6. Clarissa was paid $216 for 3 days of work. She worked 8 hours each day. Which can you use to find how much Clarissa earned per hour? Choose all that apply.
   - (A) 216 × 3 ÷ 8
   - (B) 8 × 3 ÷ 216
   - ● 216 ÷ 3 ÷ 8
   - ● 216 ÷ 8 ÷ 3

Test Tip
Multiply and divide left to right, and then, add and subtract left to right.

DIRECTIONS: Use the information below to answer Questions 7 and 8.

Jamie read for 30 minutes on Monday, 47 minutes on Tuesday, 64 minutes on Wednesday, and 81 minutes on Thursday. On Friday, Jamie spent 15 fewer minutes reading than on Monday.

7. How many total minutes did Jamie spend reading those days? Show your work.

Possible Answer:
237 minutes. First, add 30+47+64+81=222; Then, subtract 15 from 30 and add to the previous sum, 30 - 15 = 15; 222 + 15 = 237

8. How many hours and minutes is this? Show how you know.

Possible Answer: 3 hours and 57 minutes; subtract 60 from 237 three times: 237 - 60 = 177; 177 - 60 = 117; 117 - 60 = 57

9. Three friends are counting their sports cards and putting them in plastic bags to trade. Oliver has 72 cards and Casey has 56 cards. If they put them in bags of 8 cards each, how many bags will they need? Show two ways you can solve this problem.

Possible Answer: 16 bags;
one way:
72÷8+56÷8=9+7=16;
another way:
72+56 ÷8=128÷8= 16

10. In the school band, 3 rows of students play trumpet, 2 rows play trombone, and 1 row plays drums. If there are 10 students in each row, how many students are in the band?
   - (A) 50 students
   - ● 60 students
   - (C) 30 students
   - (D) 16 students

62

Find Factors and Multiples
Operations and Algebraic Thinking

DIRECTIONS: Choose or write the correct answer.

Strategy — Use factors and multiples to find the answer.

EXAMPLE
Factors are numbers multiplied together to obtain a product. A *multiple* is the product of a given whole number and any other whole number.
Factors of 36: 1, 2, 3, 4, 6, 9, 12
Some multiples of 6: 30, 36, 42, 48

1. Which shows all of the factors of 15?
   - (A) 1, 15
   - (B) 1, 3, 15
   - ● 1, 3, 5, 15
   - (D) 5, 10, 15, 20

2. All even numbers are multiples of what number?
   - (A) 1
   - ● 2
   - (C) 4
   - (D) 10

3. List all of the factor pairs of 56.
   1, 56; 2, 28; 4, 14; 7, 8

Test Tip
A prime number is a number greater than 1 that has only 2 factors: 1 and itself. Composite numbers have more than 2 factors.

4. Ginny's brother's age is a prime number between 12 and 20. Which number could be his age? Choose all that apply.
   - (A) 15
   - ● 13
   - ● 19
   - ● 17

5. **DIRECTIONS:** Use the numbers in the box to complete the table below. Some numbers may not be used. Some numbers may be used more than once.

4	8	12	16	18	48	68	96	144

Multiples of 48	Factors of 48
48, 96, 144	4, 8, 12, 16, 24, 48

6. Which are the prime number factors of 12?
   - (A) 2, 3, 4
   - (B) 24, 36, 48
   - (C) 2, 6
   - ● 1, 2, 3

7. Lucinda has 78 books on her shelves. Is 78 a prime or a composite number? Write how you know.

78 is a composite number because it is an even number, divisible by 2. It has more than two factors.

63

Analyze Patterns
Operations and Algebraic Thinking

DIRECTIONS: Choose or write the correct answer.

Strategy — Find features in the pattern to determine what comes next and to identify the rule.

EXAMPLE
What is the rule? Find the pattern in the row of numbers. Fill in the blanks with the missing numbers to complete the pattern.
64, 54, 44, ___, ___, 14, ___
Rule: Subtract 10.
Missing numbers: 34, 24, 4

1. Look at the pattern. Which shape comes next?

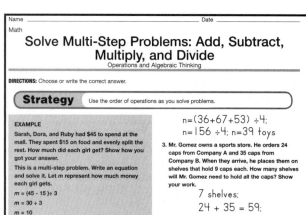

   - (A) ○
   - ● □
   - (C) △
   - (D) □

2. **DIRECTIONS:** Look for a pattern in the IN and OUT numbers in the table. Fill in the table. Then, write the rule.

IN	2	9	81	76	37	25	42
OUT	11	18	90	85	46	34	51

Rule: add 9 to the top numbers; subtract 9 from the bottom numbers.

DIRECTIONS: For Questions 3 and 4, write the missing numbers. Then, write the rule.

3. 88, ___, 66, ___, 44, ___, ___
   Missing numbers: 77, 55, 33, 22
   Rule: subtract 11

4. 17, 25, 33, ___, ___, ___
   Missing numbers: 41, 49, 57
   Rule: add 8

5. Which number pattern follows the rule "multiply by 6"?
   - (A) 6, 12, 24, 48
   - (B) 1, 7, 13, 19
   - (C) 6, 6, 12, 12
   - ● 1, 6, 36, 216

6. Start with the number 78. Write the missing numbers using the rule "add 4."
   78, 82, 86, 90, 94, 98, 102

64

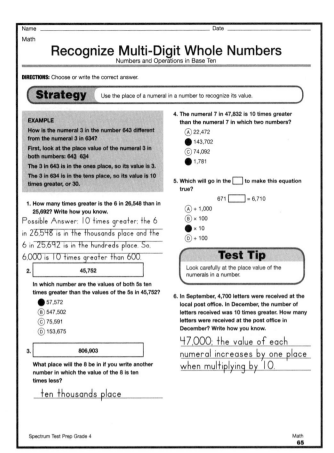

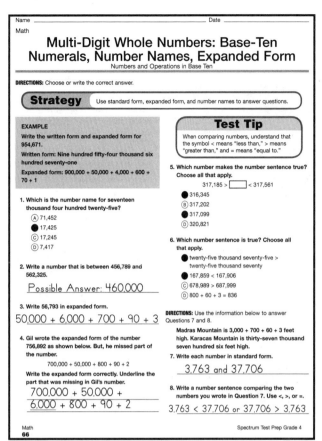

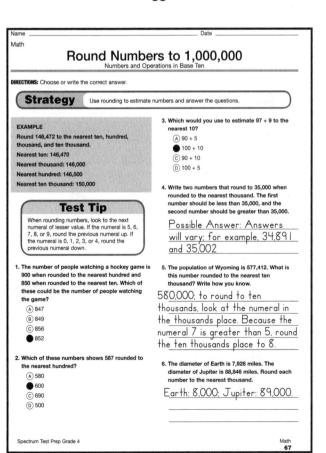

65

66

67

68

Multiply Whole Numbers Using Strategies
Numbers and Operations in Base Ten

DIRECTIONS: Choose or write the correct answer.

Strategy Use or sketch models, drawings, or numbers when multiplying.

EXAMPLE

Twenty-seven students each brought 1 dozen cookies to the class bake sale. How many cookies did they bring?

$12 \times 27 = c$

Using a place value strategy, you can reduce 12 to 10 and 2.

$227 \times 10 = 270$
$27 \times 2 = 54$
$270 + 54 = 324$

They brought 324 cookies.

DIRECTIONS: Use the information below to answer Questions 1 and 2.

Nolan gathered eggs from his chickens. He filled 43 cartons, with 12 eggs in each carton. To find the total number of eggs, Nolan first multiplied 10 by 43 and then multiplied 2 by 43.

1. What is the next step to find the total number of eggs?

Possible Answer: Add the product of 10 and 43 to the product of 2 and 43.

2. How many eggs did Nolan gather?

516 eggs

3. Sophie joined a baseball league that has 38 players. Their uniforms cost $40 each. What is the total cost of the players' uniforms? Use your understanding of place value to explain how you found your answer.

Possible Answer: One way is to multiply 38 by 10 to get 380; then, multiply 380 by 4 to get $1,520.

4. The running club is planning a bus trip to the next race. There are 64 members in the club. Each member has to pay $10 for the bus ride. How much money will the trip cost?

$640

5. Explain what happens to a value when it is multiplied by 10. Use the numbers in Question 4 in your explanation.

When you multiply 64 by 10, you add a 0 to the number; or, the value of the number becomes 10 times greater.

6. Serena solved the problem 35 × 26 this way. Show why the answer is not correct. Include the correct answer.

```
   26
 × 35
  130
 + 78
  208
```

Possible Answer: The first partial product is correct. The second partial product needs to start in the tens column under the 1, not the ones column under the 0. The correct answer is 910.

Multiply Whole Numbers Using Strategies
Numbers and Operations in Base Ten

DIRECTIONS: Choose or write the correct answer.

Strategy Multiply whole numbers using strategies based on place value and properties of operations.

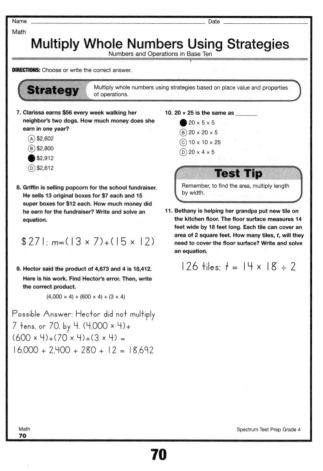

7. Clarissa earns $56 every week walking her neighbor's two dogs. How much money does she earn in one year?

Ⓐ $2,602
Ⓑ $2,800
● $2,912
Ⓓ $2,612

8. Griffin is selling popcorn for the school fundraiser. He sells 13 original boxes for $7 each and 15 super boxes for $12 each. How much money did he earn for the fundraiser? Write and solve an equation.

$271; $m=(13 \times 7)+(15 \times 12)$

9. Hector said the product of 4,673 and 4 is 18,412. Here is his work. Find Hector's error. Then, write the correct product.

$(4,000 \times 4) + (600 \times 4) + (3 \times 4)$

Possible Answer: Hector did not multiply 7 tens, or 70, by 4. $(4,000 \times 4) + (600 \times 4) + (70 \times 4) + (3 \times 4) = 16,000 + 2,400 + 280 + 12 = 18,692$

10. 20 × 25 is the same as _____

● 20 × 5 × 5
Ⓑ 20 × 20 × 5
Ⓒ 10 × 10 × 25
Ⓓ 20 × 4 × 5

Test Tip
Remember, to find the area, multiply length by width.

11. Bethany is helping her grandpa put new tile on the kitchen floor. The floor surface measures 14 feet wide by 18 feet long. Each tile can cover an area of 2 square feet. How many tiles, t, will they need to cover the floor surface? Write and solve an equation.

126 tiles; $t = 14 \times 18 \div 2$

Divide Whole Numbers Using Strategies
Numbers and Operations in Base Ten

DIRECTIONS: Choose or write the correct answer.

Strategy Divide whole numbers using strategies based on place value and properties of operations.

EXAMPLE

Mr. Larson has a vegetable garden. There are a total of 294 vegetable plants in 7 rows, with an equal number of plants in each row. How many plants are in each of the 7 rows in Mr. Larson's garden?

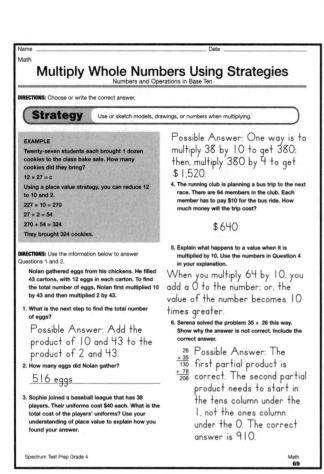

294 plants

Divide to find the answer. $294 \div 7 = 42$
There are 42 plants in each row.

1. Ken works 8 hours a day at the widget factory. He assembles the same number of widgets every hour. If he assembles 1,752 widgets a day, how many widgets does he assemble per hour?

Ⓐ 200
● 219
Ⓒ 209
Ⓓ 305

2. Jacob has a bag with 124 game tokens. His father puts 68 more tokens into the bag. Jacob now shares the tokens with 3 friends. How many tokens, t, do Jacob and his friends each receive? Write an equation. Then, solve it.

48 tokens; $t = (124 + 68) \div 4$;
$192 \div 4 = 48$

3. There are 3 sports stadiums in the city where Tomas lives. One weekend, a total of 6,693 people watched events at the 3 stadiums. The same number of people were at each stadium. Which equation can be used to find how many people were at each stadium?

● $(6,000 \div 3) + (600 \div 3) + (90 \div 3) + (3 \div 3) = \square$
Ⓑ $(6,000 \div 3) + (600 \div 3) + (90 \div 3) + (30 \div 3) = \square$
Ⓒ $(6,000 \div 3) + (60 \div 3) + (90 \div 3) + (3 \div 3) = \square$
Ⓓ $(6,000 \div 3) + (600 \div 3) + (900 \div 3) + (3 \div 3) = \square$

Test Tip
Use models or drawings to help when dividing.

4. Which array correctly represents 79 ÷ 5?

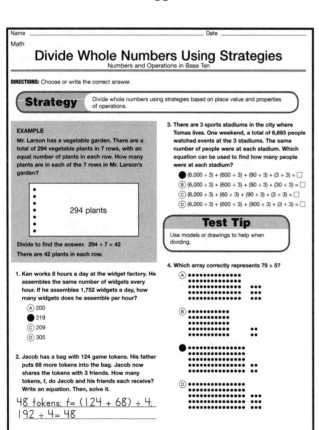

Divide Whole Numbers Using Strategies
Numbers and Operations in Base Ten

DIRECTIONS: Choose or write the correct answer.

Strategy Remember how multiplication and division relate to help you solve division problems.

DIRECTIONS: Use the information below to answer Questions 5 and 6.

Remy solved the problem 672 ÷ 6. These are the steps she did to solve it.

- First, she found how many times 6 can go into 6 hundreds.
- Then, she found how many times 6 can go into 7 tens.
- Finally, she found how many times 6 can go into 2 ones.

5. Is Remy correct? Tell why or why not.

Possible Answer: No, Remy is not correct. In the last step, she should find how many times 6 goes into 12 ones, not 2 ones.

6. Solve the problem. Show your work.

112

7. Jessie earned $574 for mowing his neighbor's lawn for 7 weeks during the summer. She earned the same amount each week. Which equation correctly shows how much money Jessie earned per week?

Ⓐ $574 \div 7 = 820$
Ⓑ $574 \div 7 = 182$
● $574 \div 7 = 82$
Ⓓ $574 \div 7 = 802$

Test Tip
You can check your answers in a division problem by multiplying the quotient by the divisor.

8. Luis organizes books in the school library. He wants to place 135 books in equal stacks of 9 books each.

He does the division problem below to find how many books will be in each stack.

$135 \div 9 = 15$

Write an equation Luis can use to check his division.

$15 \times 9 = \square$

9. Look at the division problem below.

$335 \div 5$

Use words or numbers to explain how you can break apart 335 to make the division easier. Be sure to include the quotient in your explanation.

Possible Answer: Break apart 335 into 300 + 35. Then, divide each part by 5: $300 \div 5 = 60$ and $35 \div 5 = 7$. Finally, add to get the quotient: $60 + 7 = 67$

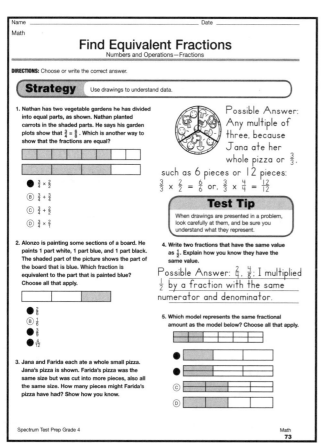

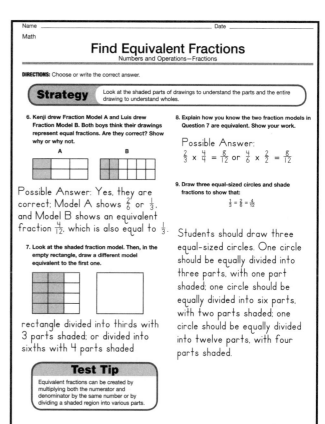

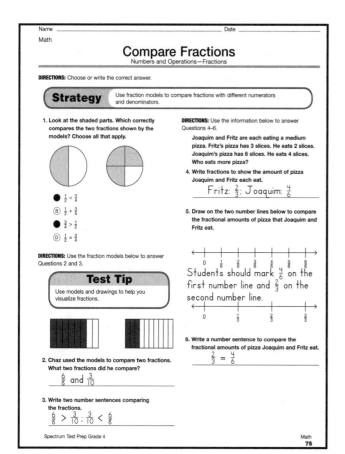

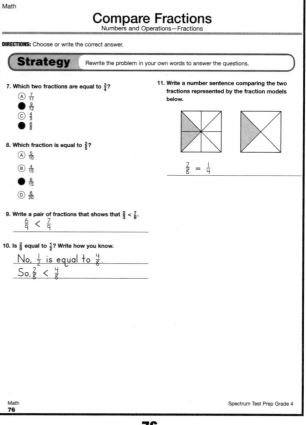

Compose and Decompose Fractions
Numbers and Operations—Fractions

DIRECTIONS: Choose or write the correct answer.

Strategy Compose and decompose fractions using addition.

1. Which format shows the sum of $\frac{3}{4}$? Choose all that apply.
   - ● $\frac{1}{4} + \frac{1}{4} + \frac{1}{4}$
   - Ⓑ $\frac{1}{4} + \frac{3}{4}$
   - ● $\frac{1}{4} + \frac{2}{4}$
   - Ⓓ $\frac{1}{4} + \frac{1}{4} + \frac{2}{4}$

2. Which expression does not have a value of 1?
   - Ⓐ $\frac{7}{12} + \frac{5}{12}$
   - ● $\frac{4}{12} + \frac{10}{12}$
   - Ⓒ $\frac{4}{12} + \frac{8}{12}$
   - Ⓓ $\frac{1}{12} + \frac{1}{12} + \frac{10}{12}$

Test Tip
Pay close attention to the numbers in the problem and the answer choices. If you misread even one number, you may choose the wrong answer.

3. Lacy drew the fraction model below to help her add fractions. Write the equation shown by her model.

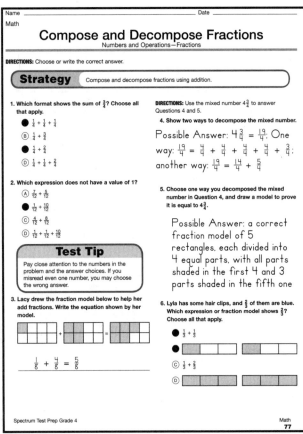

$\frac{1}{8} + \frac{4}{8} = \frac{5}{8}$

DIRECTIONS: Use the mixed number $4\frac{3}{4}$ to answer Questions 4 and 5.

4. Show two ways to decompose the mixed number.

Possible Answer: $4\frac{3}{4} = \frac{19}{4}$. One way: $\frac{19}{4} = \frac{4}{4} + \frac{4}{4} + \frac{4}{4} + \frac{4}{4} + \frac{3}{4}$; another way: $\frac{19}{4} = \frac{14}{4} + \frac{5}{4}$

5. Choose one way you decomposed the mixed number in Question 4, and draw a model to prove it is equal to $4\frac{3}{4}$.

Possible Answer: a correct fraction model of 5 rectangles, each divided into 4 equal parts, with all parts shaded in the first 4 and 3 parts shaded in the fifth one

6. Lyla has some hair clips, and $\frac{2}{3}$ of them are blue. Which expression or fraction model shows $\frac{2}{3}$? Choose all that apply.
   - ● $\frac{1}{3} + \frac{1}{3}$
   - ● [fraction model]
   - Ⓒ $\frac{1}{3} + \frac{2}{3}$
   - Ⓓ [fraction model]

77

Compose and Decompose Fractions
Numbers and Operations—Fractions

DIRECTIONS: Choose or write the correct answer.

Strategy Use visuals when composing and decomposing fractions. Draw boxes to equal the denominator. Then, shade in boxes that equal the numerator. Use different colors for each fraction.

Test Tip When decomposing fractions using addition, use the same denominator.

7. Which is a correct way to write $1\frac{6}{8}$ as a sum of fractions?
   - Ⓐ $\frac{8}{8} + \frac{8}{8} + \frac{8}{8} + \frac{8}{8} + \frac{8}{8} + \frac{1}{1}$
   - ● $\frac{8}{8} + \frac{1}{8} + \frac{5}{8}$
   - Ⓒ $\frac{8}{8} + \frac{1}{8}$
   - Ⓓ $\frac{8}{8} + \frac{9}{8}$

Test Tip
Before you choose an answer, ask yourself, "Does this answer make sense?"

8. Jerrod shaded a shape as shown below.

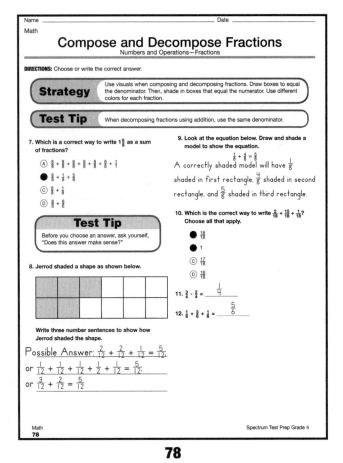

Write three number sentences to show how Jerrod shaded the shape.

Possible Answer: $\frac{2}{12} + \frac{2}{12} + \frac{1}{12} = \frac{5}{12}$;
or $\frac{1}{12} + \frac{1}{12} + \frac{1}{12} + \frac{1}{12} + \frac{1}{12} = \frac{5}{12}$;
or $\frac{3}{12} + \frac{2}{12} = \frac{5}{12}$

9. Look at the equation below. Draw and shade a model to show the equation.

$\frac{1}{8} + \frac{4}{8} + \frac{5}{8}$

A correctly shaded model will have $\frac{1}{8}$ shaded in first rectangle, $\frac{4}{8}$ shaded in second rectangle, and $\frac{5}{8}$ shaded in third rectangle.

10. Which is the correct way to write $\frac{2}{18} + \frac{15}{18} + \frac{1}{18}$? Choose all that apply.
   - ● $\frac{18}{18}$
   - ● 1
   - Ⓒ $\frac{17}{18}$
   - Ⓓ $\frac{16}{18}$

11. $\frac{3}{4} - \frac{2}{4} = \underline{\quad \frac{1}{4} \quad}$

12. $\frac{1}{8} + \frac{3}{8} + \frac{1}{8} = \underline{\quad \frac{5}{6} \quad}$

78

Add and Subtract Mixed Numbers
Numbers and Operations—Fractions

DIRECTIONS: Choose or write the correct answer.

Strategy Use equivalent fractions to add and subtract mixed numbers with like denominators.

1. Which is the sum of $1\frac{2}{4} + 2\frac{1}{4}$?
   - Ⓐ $\frac{4}{3}$
   - ● $3\frac{3}{4}$
   - Ⓒ $2\frac{3}{4}$
   - Ⓓ $1\frac{3}{4}$

2. The Spencer family went on a trip. It took them $1\frac{1}{6}$ hours the first day and $2\frac{4}{6}$ hours the next day to get to their destination. What is the total time for their trip? Show your work.

$1\frac{1}{6} + 2\frac{4}{6} = 3\frac{5}{6}$ hours

3. Bianca has $3\frac{4}{8}$ pizzas left over from her party. She takes some pizza to her friend's house the next day and leaves $1\frac{3}{8}$ pizzas at home. How much pizza did Bianca take to her friend's house?
   - ● $2\frac{1}{8}$ pizzas
   - Ⓑ $4\frac{7}{8}$ pizzas
   - Ⓒ $4\frac{1}{8}$ pizza
   - Ⓓ $1\frac{1}{8}$ pizza

4. Look at the equation below.
$1\frac{3}{8} - \frac{3}{8} = n$

What is true about n in the following number sentences? Choose all that apply.
   - ● $\frac{8}{8} - \frac{3}{8} = n$
   - ● $n + \frac{3}{8} = 1\frac{3}{8}$
   - Ⓒ $n - 1\frac{3}{8} = \frac{3}{8}$
   - ● $n = \frac{8}{8}$

Test Tip
Look carefully at every answer choice. Then, choose the one that best answers the problem.

5. Add. Show your work.
$4\frac{5}{6} + 3\frac{2}{6}$

Possible Answer:
$4\frac{5}{6} + 3\frac{2}{6} = 7\frac{7}{6}$ or $7\frac{1}{3}$

79

Add and Subtract Mixed Numbers
Numbers and Operations—Fractions

DIRECTIONS: Choose or write the correct answer.

Strategy Use addition and subtraction of mixed numbers with like denominators to solve real-world problems.

6. Raj wants to solve this number sentence, but he doesn't know where to begin.

$2\frac{4}{12} - \frac{7}{12} = \square$

Use words or numbers to help Raj solve the problem. Include the difference in your explanation.

Possible Answer: Change $2\frac{4}{12}$ to an improper fraction: $12 \times 2 + 4 = \frac{28}{12}$. Then, subtract $\frac{7}{12}$ from $\frac{28}{12}$ to get $\frac{21}{12}$, or $\frac{7}{4}$.

7. Inga had $2\frac{3}{4}$ granola bars. She ate $\frac{2}{4}$ of them at snack time. How much was left for her to eat after school? Show your work.

$2\frac{1}{4}$ granola bars were left:
$2\frac{3}{4} - \frac{2}{4} = 2\frac{1}{4}$ or $\frac{11}{4} - \frac{2}{4} = \frac{9}{4} = 2\frac{1}{4}$

8. Rachel is making doll clothes for her younger sister's doll. She has a total of $4\frac{5}{8}$ yards of cloth. She uses $1\frac{3}{8}$ yards to make dresses and $\frac{4}{8}$ yard to make pants. How much cloth does she have left to make shirts? Show how you found your answer.

Possible Answer:
$2\frac{6}{8}$ yd. $1\frac{3}{8} + \frac{4}{8} = 1\frac{7}{8}$. Then, subtract $4\frac{5}{8} - 1\frac{7}{8} = \frac{37}{8} - \frac{15}{8} = \frac{22}{8}$ = or $2\frac{6}{8}$ yd

9. Dominic was watering the school garden. He started with 8 gallons of water. He used $3\frac{3}{4}$ gallons to water the tomatoes and $2\frac{1}{4}$ gallons to water the sunflowers. How many gallons of water did he have left? Show your work.

2 gallons were left:
$8 - 3\frac{3}{4} - 2\frac{1}{4} = \frac{32}{4} - \frac{15}{4} - \frac{9}{4} = \frac{8}{4}$ or 2

10. Nico needs 5 cups of flour for his bread recipe. He only has $3\frac{1}{4}$ cups of flour. How much more flour does Nico need? Show how you found your answer.

Nico needs $1\frac{3}{4}$ cups of flour:
$5 - 3\frac{1}{4} = \frac{20}{4} - \frac{13}{4} = \frac{7}{4} = 1\frac{3}{4}$

80

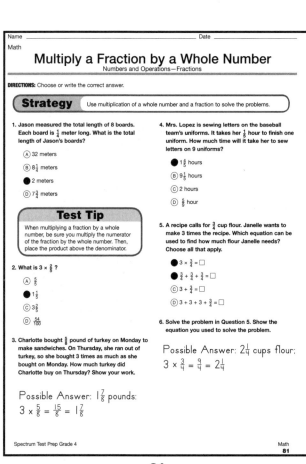

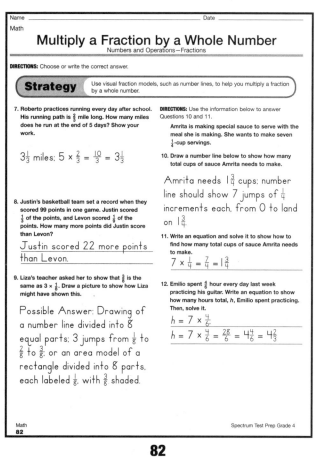

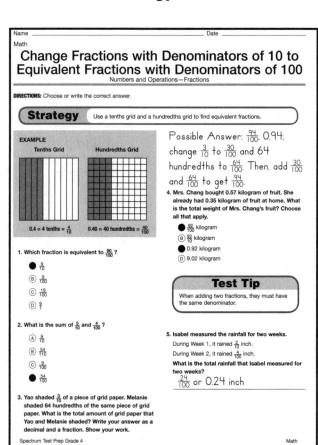

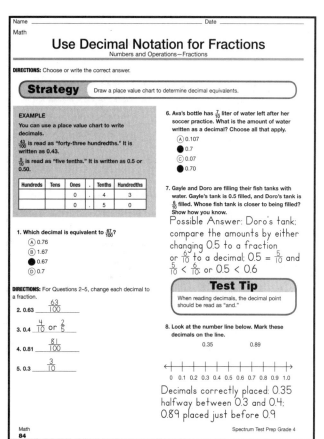

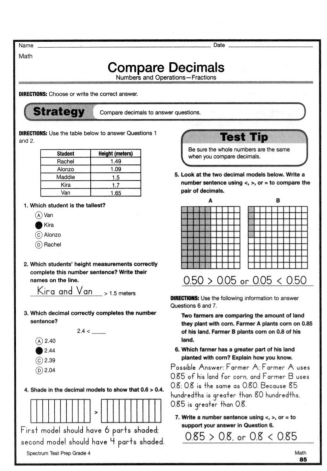

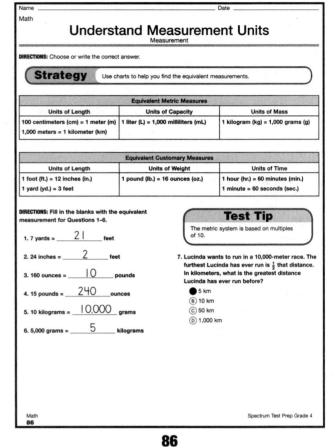

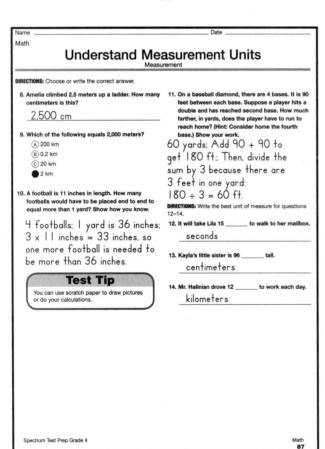

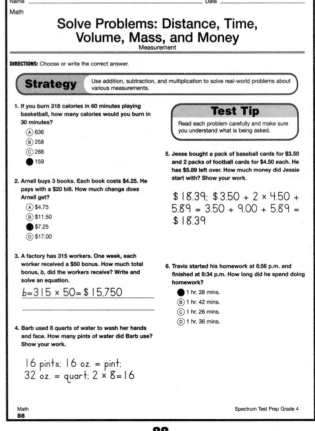

Name Date

Math

Compare Decimals

Numbers and Operations—Fractions

DIRECTIONS: Choose or write the correct answer.

Strategy Compare decimals to answer questions.

DIRECTIONS: Use the table below to answer Questions 1 and 2.

Student	Height (meters)
Rachel	1.49
Alonzo	1.09
Maddie	1.5
Kira	1.7
Van	1.65

1. Which student is the tallest?

Ⓐ Van
● Kira
Ⓒ Alonzo
Ⓓ Rachel

2. Which students' height measurements correctly complete this number sentence? Write their names on the line.

Kira and Van > 1.5 meters

3. Which decimal correctly completes the number sentence?

2.4 < ____

Ⓐ 2.40
● 2.44
Ⓒ 2.39
Ⓓ 2.04

4. Shade in the decimal models to show that 0.6 > 0.4.

First model should have 6 parts shaded; second model should have 4 parts shaded.

Test Tip

Be sure the whole numbers are the same when you compare decimals.

5. Look at the two decimal models below. Write a number sentence using <, >, or = to compare the pair of decimals.

0.50 > 0.05 or 0.05 < 0.50

DIRECTIONS: Use the following information to answer Questions 6 and 7.

Two farmers are comparing the amount of land they plant with corn. Farmer A plants corn on 0.85 of his land. Farmer B plants corn on 0.8 of his land.

6. Which farmer has a greater part of his land planted with corn? Explain how you know.

Possible Answer: Farmer A; Farmer A uses 0.85 of his land for corn, and Farmer B uses 0.8; 0.8 is the same as 0.80. Because 85 hundredths is greater than 80 hundredths, 0.85 is greater than 0.8.

7. Write a number sentence using <, >, or = to support your answer in Question 6.

0.85 > 0.8, or 0.8 < 0.85

Name Date

Math

Understand Measurement Units

Measurement

DIRECTIONS: Choose or write the correct answer.

Strategy Use charts to help you find the equivalent measurements.

Equivalent Metric Measures		
Units of Length	**Units of Capacity**	**Units of Mass**
100 centimeters (cm) = 1 meter (m) **1,000 meters = 1 kilometer (km)**	**1 liter (L) = 1,000 milliliters (mL)**	**1 kilogram (kg) = 1,000 grams (g)**

Equivalent Customary Measures		
Units of Length	**Units of Weight**	**Units of Time**
1 foot (ft.) = 12 inches (in.) **1 yard (yd.) = 3 feet**	**1 pound (lb.) = 16 ounces (oz.)**	**1 hour (hr.) = 60 minutes (min.)** **1 minute = 60 seconds (sec.)**

DIRECTIONS: Fill in the blanks with the equivalent measurement for Questions 1–6.

1. 7 yards = 21 **feet**

2. 24 inches = 2 **feet**

3. 160 ounces = 10 **pounds**

4. 15 pounds = 240 **ounces**

5. 10 kilograms = 10,000 **grams**

6. 5,000 grams = 5 **kilograms**

Test Tip

The metric system is based on multiples of 10.

7. Lucinda wants to run in a 10,000-meter race. The furthest Lucinda has ever run is $\frac{1}{2}$ that distance. In kilometers, what is the greatest distance Lucinda has ever run before?

● 5 km
Ⓑ 10 km
Ⓒ 50 km
Ⓓ 1,000 km

Name Date

Math

Understand Measurement Units

Measurement

DIRECTIONS: Choose or write the correct answer.

8. Amelia climbed 2.5 meters up a ladder. How many centimeters is this?

2,500 cm

9. Which of the following equals 2,000 meters?

Ⓐ 200 km
Ⓑ 0.2 km
Ⓒ 20 km
● 2 km

10. A football is 11 inches in length. How many footballs would have to be placed end to end to equal more than 1 yard? Show how you know.

4 footballs; 1 yard is 36 inches; 3 x 11 inches = 33 inches, so one more football is needed to be more than 36 inches.

Test Tip

You can use scratch paper to draw pictures or do your calculations.

11. On a baseball diamond, there are 4 bases. It is 90 feet between each base. Suppose a player hits a double and has reached second base. How much farther, in yards, does the player have to run to reach home? (Hint: Consider home the fourth base.) Show your work.

60 yards; Add 90 + 90 to get 180 ft.; Then, divide the sum by 3 because there are 3 feet in one yard: 180 ÷ 3 = 60 ft.

DIRECTIONS: Write the best unit of measure for questions 12–14.

12. It will take Lila 15 ______ to walk to her mailbox.

seconds

13. Kayla's little sister is 96 ______ tall.

centimeters

14. Mr. Halinian drove 12 ______ to work each day.

kilometers

Name Date

Math

Solve Problems: Distance, Time, Volume, Mass, and Money

Measurement

DIRECTIONS: Choose or write the correct answer.

Strategy Use addition, subtraction, and multiplication to solve real-world problems about various measurements.

1. If you burn 318 calories in 60 minutes playing basketball, how many calories would you burn in 30 minutes?

Ⓐ 636
Ⓑ 258
Ⓒ 288
● 159

2. Arnell buys 3 books. Each book costs $4.25. He pays with a $20 bill. How much change does Arnell get?

Ⓐ $4.75
Ⓑ $11.50
● $7.25
Ⓓ $17.00

3. A factory has 315 workers. One week, each worker received a $50 bonus. How much total bonus, *b*, did the workers receive? Write and solve an equation.

b=315 x 50= $15,750

4. Barb used 8 quarts of water to wash her hands and face. How many pints of water did Barb use? Show your work.

16 pints; 16 oz. = pint; 32 oz. = quart; 2 x 8=16

Test Tip

Read each problem carefully and make sure you understand what is being asked.

5. Jesse bought a pack of baseball cards for $3.50 and 2 packs of football cards for $4.50 each. He has $5.89 left over. How much money did Jessie start with? Show your work.

$18.39; $3.50 + 2 x 4.50 + 5.89 = 3.50 + 9.00 + 5.89 = $18.39

6. Travis started his homework at 6:56 p.m. and finished at 8:34 p.m. How long did he spend doing homework?

● 1 hr. 38 mins.
Ⓑ 1 hr. 42 mins.
Ⓒ 1 hr. 26 mins.
Ⓓ 1 hr. 36 mins.

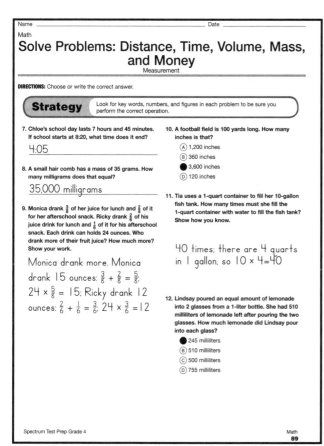

Solve Problems: Distance, Time, Volume, Mass, and Money
Measurement

DIRECTIONS: Choose or write the correct answer.

Strategy Look for key words, numbers, and figures in each problem to be sure you perform the correct operation.

7. Chloe's school day lasts 7 hours and 45 minutes. If school starts at 8:20, what time does it end?

4:05

8. A small hair comb has a mass of 35 grams. How many milligrams does that equal?

35,000 milligrams

9. Monica drank $\frac{3}{8}$ of her juice for lunch and $\frac{2}{8}$ of it for her afterschool snack. Ricky drank $\frac{2}{6}$ of his juice drink for lunch and $\frac{1}{6}$ of it for his afterschool snack. Each drink can holds 24 ounces. Who drank more of their fruit juice? How much more? Show your work.

Monica drank more. Monica drank 15 ounces: $\frac{3}{8} + \frac{2}{8} = \frac{5}{8}$; $24 \times \frac{5}{8} = 15$; Ricky drank 12 ounces: $\frac{2}{6} + \frac{1}{6} = \frac{3}{6}$; $24 \times \frac{3}{6} = 12$

10. A football field is 100 yards long. How many inches is that?
- (A) 1,200 inches
- (B) 360 inches
- (●) 3,600 inches
- (D) 120 inches

11. Tia uses a 1-quart container to fill her 10-gallon fish tank. How many times must she fill the 1-quart container with water to fill the fish tank? Show how you know.

40 times; there are 4 quarts in 1 gallon, so $10 \times 4 = 40$

12. Lindsay poured an equal amount of lemonade into 2 glasses from a 1-liter bottle. She had 510 milliliters of lemonade left after pouring the two glasses. How much lemonade did Lindsay pour into each glass?
- (●) 245 milliliters
- (B) 510 milliliters
- (C) 500 milliliters
- (D) 755 milliliters

89

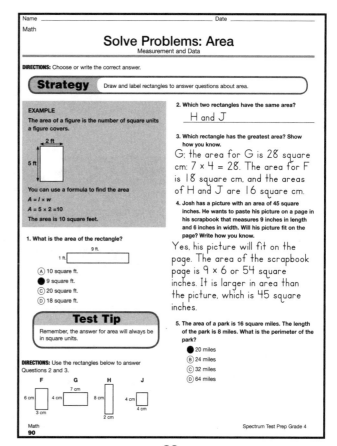

Solve Problems: Area
Measurement and Data

DIRECTIONS: Choose or write the correct answer.

Strategy Draw and label rectangles to answer questions about area.

EXAMPLE
The area of a figure is the number of square units a figure covers.

2 ft
5 ft

You can use a formula to find the area
$A = l \times w$
$A = 5 \times 2 = 10$
The area is 10 square feet.

1. What is the area of the rectangle?

9 ft.
1 ft.
- (A) 10 square ft.
- (●) 9 square ft.
- (C) 20 square ft.
- (D) 18 square ft.

Test Tip
Remember, the answer for area will always be in square units.

DIRECTIONS: Use the rectangles below to answer Questions 2 and 3.

F 6 cm, 3 cm
G 7 cm, 4 cm
H 8 cm, 2 cm
J 4 cm, 4 cm

2. Which two rectangles have the same area?

H and J

3. Which rectangle has the greatest area? Show how you know.

G; the area for G is 28 square cm: $7 \times 4 = 28$. The area for F is 18 square cm, and the areas of H and J are 16 square cm.

4. Josh has a picture with an area of 45 square inches. He wants to paste his picture on a page in his scrapbook that measures 9 inches in length and 6 inches in width. Will his picture fit on the page? Write how you know.

Yes, his picture will fit on the page. The area of the scrapbook page is 9×6 or 54 square inches. It is larger in area than the picture, which is 45 square inches.

5. The area of a park is 16 square miles. The length of the park is 8 miles. What is the perimeter of the park?
- (●) 20 miles
- (B) 24 miles
- (C) 32 miles
- (D) 64 miles

90

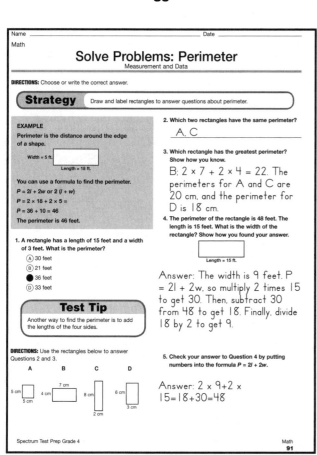

Solve Problems: Perimeter
Measurement and Data

DIRECTIONS: Choose or write the correct answer.

Strategy Draw and label rectangles to answer questions about perimeter.

EXAMPLE
Perimeter is the distance around the edge of a shape.

Width = 5 ft.
Length = 18 ft.

You can use a formula to find the perimeter.
$P = 2l + 2w$ or $2 (l + w)$
$P = 2 \times 18 + 2 \times 5 =$
$P = 36 + 10 = 46$
The perimeter is 46 feet.

1. A rectangle has a length of 15 feet and a width of 3 feet. What is the perimeter?
- (A) 30 feet
- (B) 21 feet
- (●) 36 feet
- (D) 33 feet

Test Tip
Another way to find the perimeter is to add the lengths of the four sides.

DIRECTIONS: Use the rectangles below to answer Questions 2 and 3.

A 5 cm, 5 cm
B 7 cm, 4 cm
C 8 cm, 2 cm
D 6 cm, 3 cm

2. Which two rectangles have the same perimeter?

A, C

3. Which rectangle has the greatest perimeter? Show how you know.

B; $2 \times 7 + 2 \times 4 = 22$. The perimeters for A and C are 20 cm, and the perimeter for D is 18 cm.

4. The perimeter of the rectangle is 48 feet. The length is 15 feet. What is the width of the rectangle? Show how you found your answer.

Length = 15 ft.

Answer: The width is 9 feet. $P = 2l + 2w$, so multiply 2 times 15 to get 30. Then, subtract 30 from 48 to get 18. Finally, divide 18 by 2 to get 9.

5. Check your answer to Question 4 by putting numbers into the formula $P = 2l + 2w$.

Answer: $2 \times 9 + 2 \times 15 = 18 + 30 = 48$

91

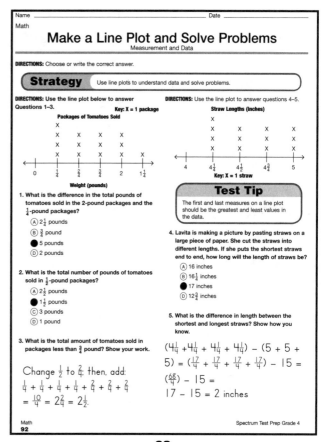

Make a Line Plot and Solve Problems
Measurement and Data

DIRECTIONS: Choose or write the correct answer.

Strategy Use line plots to understand data and solve problems.

DIRECTIONS: Use the line plot below to answer Questions 1–3.

Key: X = 1 package
Packages of Tomatoes Sold

0    $\frac{1}{4}$ $\frac{2}{4}$ $\frac{3}{4}$ 2   1$\frac{1}{4}$
Weight (pounds)

1. What is the difference in the total pounds of tomatoes sold in the 2-pound packages and the $\frac{1}{4}$-pound packages?
- (A) 2$\frac{1}{4}$ pounds
- (B) $\frac{3}{4}$ pound
- (●) 5 pounds
- (D) 2 pounds

2. What is the total number of pounds of tomatoes sold in $\frac{1}{2}$-pound packages?
- (A) 2$\frac{1}{2}$ pounds
- (●) 1$\frac{1}{2}$ pounds
- (C) 3 pounds
- (D) 1 pound

3. What is the total amount of tomatoes sold in packages less than $\frac{3}{4}$ pound? Show your work.

Change $\frac{1}{2}$ to $\frac{2}{4}$, then, add: $\frac{1}{4} + \frac{1}{4} + \frac{1}{4} + \frac{1}{4} + \frac{2}{4} + \frac{2}{4} = \frac{10}{4} = 2\frac{2}{4} = 2\frac{1}{2}$.

DIRECTIONS: Use the line plot to answer questions 4–5.

Straw Lengths (inches)
4    $4\frac{1}{4}$ $4\frac{2}{4}$ $4\frac{3}{4}$ 5
Key: X = 1 straw

Test Tip
The first and last measures on a line plot should be the greatest and least values in the data.

4. Lavita is making a picture by pasting straws on a large piece of paper. She cut the straws into different lengths. If she puts the shortest straws end to end, how long will the length of straws be?
- (A) 16 inches
- (B) 16$\frac{1}{4}$ inches
- (●) 17 inches
- (D) 12$\frac{3}{4}$ inches

5. What is the difference in length between the shortest and longest straws? Show how you know.

$(4\frac{1}{4} + 4\frac{1}{4} + 4\frac{1}{4} + 4\frac{1}{4}) - (5 + 5 + 5) = (\frac{17}{4} + \frac{17}{4} + \frac{17}{4} + \frac{17}{4}) - 15 = (\frac{68}{4}) - 15 = 17 - 15 = 2$ inches

92

Understand Angle Concepts and Measurement
Measurement and Data

DIRECTIONS: Choose or write the correct answer.

Strategy Use drawings or sketches to answer questions about angle measurement.

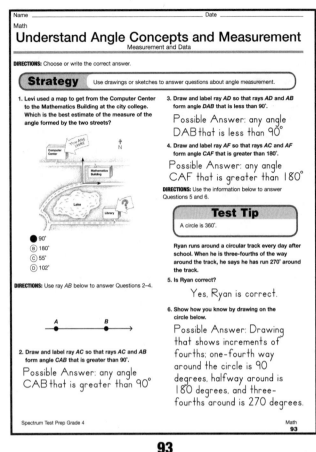

1. Levi used a map to get from the Computer Center to the Mathematics Building at the city college. Which is the best estimate of the measure of the angle formed by the two streets?

● 90°
Ⓑ 180°
Ⓒ 55°
Ⓓ 102°

DIRECTIONS: Use ray *AB* below to answer Questions 2–4.

2. Draw and label ray *AC* so that rays *AC* and *AB* form angle *CAB* that is greater than 90°.

Possible Answer: any angle CAB that is greater than 90°

3. Draw and label ray *AD* so that rays *AD* and *AB* form angle *DAB* that is less than 90°.

Possible Answer: any angle DAB that is less than 90°

4. Draw and label ray *AF* so that rays *AC* and *AF* form angle *CAF* that is greater than 180°.

Possible Answer: any angle CAF that is greater than 180°

DIRECTIONS: Use the information below to answer Questions 5 and 6.

Test Tip
A circle is 360°.

Ryan runs around a circular track every day after school. When he is three-fourths of the way around the track, he says he has run 270° around the track.

5. Is Ryan correct?

Yes, Ryan is correct.

6. Show how you know by drawing on the circle below.

Possible Answer: Drawing that shows increments of fourths; one-fourth way around the circle is 90 degrees, halfway around is 180 degrees, and three-fourths around is 270 degrees.

Spectrum Test Prep Grade 4

Math 93

93

Measuring Angles
Geometry

DIRECTIONS: Choose or write the correct answer.

Strategy Use a protractor to answer questions about angle measurement.

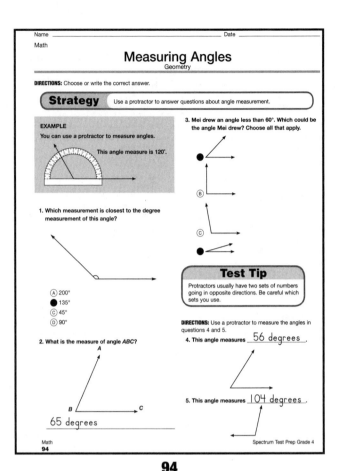

EXAMPLE
You can use a protractor to measure angles.
This angle measure is 120°.

1. Which measurement is closest to the degree measurement of this angle?

Ⓐ 200°
● 135°
Ⓒ 45°
Ⓓ 90°

2. What is the measure of angle *ABC*?

65 degrees

3. Mei drew an angle less than 60°. Which could be the angle Mei drew? Choose all that apply.

Test Tip
Protractors usually have two sets of numbers going in opposite directions. Be careful which sets you use.

DIRECTIONS: Use a protractor to measure the angles in questions 4 and 5.

4. This angle measures __56 degrees__.

5. This angle measures __104 degrees__.

Spectrum Test Prep Grade 4

Math 94

94

Solve Problems: Unknown Angle Measures
Geometry

DIRECTIONS: Choose or write the correct answer.

Strategy Solve unknown measures by using the properties of angles.

EXAMPLE
The angle measures in a triangle always equal 180°. The angle measures in any quadrilateral always equal 360°.

What is the measure of angle *A*?

Answer: The measure is 60 degrees because 180 – (30 + 90) = 60.

Test Tip
The angle measure of the whole is the sum of the angle measures of all the parts.

DIRECTIONS: Use the figures below to answer questions 3 and 4.

Figure A   **Figure B**

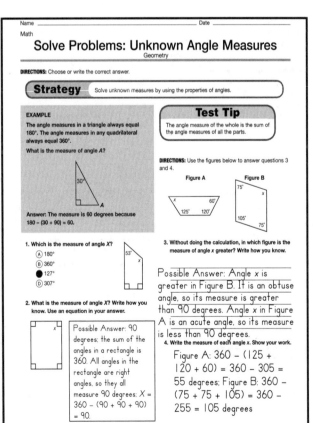

1. Which is the measure of angle *X*?

Ⓐ 180°
Ⓑ 360°
● 127°
Ⓓ 307°

2. What is the measure of angle *X*? Write how you know. Use an equation in your answer.

Possible Answer: 90 degrees; the sum of the angles in a rectangle is 360. All angles in the rectangle are right angles, so they all measure 90 degrees; X = 360 – (90 + 90 + 90) = 90.

3. Without doing the calculation, in which figure is the measure of angle *x* greater? Write how you know.

Possible Answer: Angle x is greater in Figure B. It is an obtuse angle, so its measure is greater than 90 degrees. Angle x in Figure A is an acute angle, so its measure is less than 90 degrees.

4. Write the measure of each angle *x*. Show your work.

Figure A: 360 – (125 + 120 + 60) = 360 – 305 = 55 degrees; Figure B: 360 – (75 + 75 + 105) = 360 – 255 = 105 degrees

Spectrum Test Prep Grade 4

Math 95

95

Solve Problems: Unknown Angle Measures
Geometry

DIRECTIONS: Choose or write the correct answer.

Strategy Use the drawings and labels to understand which angle measurement to find.

DIRECTIONS: Use the image below to answer Questions 5 and 6.

5. What is the measure of angle *H*?

Ⓐ 45°
Ⓑ 180°
● 135°
Ⓓ 65°

6. Write how you found your answer in Question 5.

Possible Answer: A straight line measures 180 degrees; subtract 45 degrees from 180 to get 135.

Test Tip
The sum of the angles of a circle is 360°.

7. At 3:00, the hands on the clock form a 90° angle. What angle will they be at 6:00?

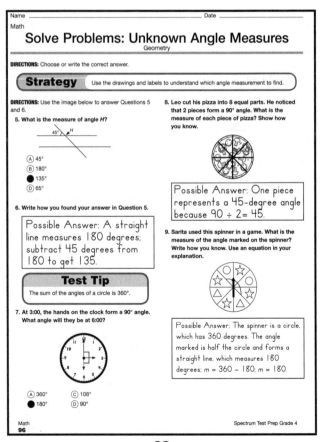

Ⓐ 360°   Ⓒ 108°
● 180°   Ⓓ 90°

8. Leo cut his pizza into 8 equal parts. He noticed that 2 pieces form a 90° angle. What is the measure of each piece of pizza? Show how you know.

Possible Answer: One piece represents a 45-degree angle because 90 ÷ 2 = 45.

9. Sarita used this spinner in a game. What is the measure of the angle marked on the spinner? Write how you know. Use an equation in your explanation.

Possible Answer: The spinner is a circle, which has 360 degrees. The angle marked is half the circle and forms a straight line, which measures 180 degrees; m = 360 – 180; m = 180.

Math 96

Spectrum Test Prep Grade 4

96

Identify Lines and Angles
Geometry

DIRECTIONS: Choose or write the correct answer.

Strategy Use the properties of lines and angles to answer the questions.

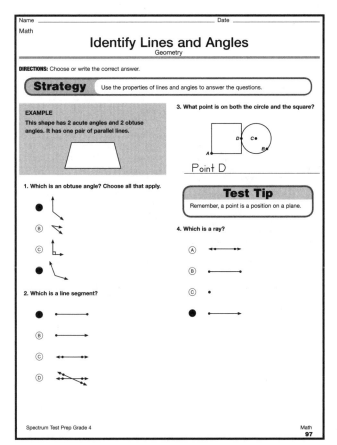

EXAMPLE
This shape has 2 acute angles and 2 obtuse angles. It has one pair of parallel lines.

1. Which is an obtuse angle? Choose all that apply.

● A
B
C
● D

2. Which is a line segment?

● A
B
C
D

3. What point is on both the circle and the square?

Point D

Test Tip
Remember, a point is a position on a plane.

4. Which is a ray?

A
B
C
●

97

Solve Problems: Unknown Angle Measures
Geometry

DIRECTIONS: Choose or write the correct answer.

Strategy Use what you know about the types of angles and their measurements to solve unknown measures.

DIRECTIONS: Use the shape below to answer questions 1–5.

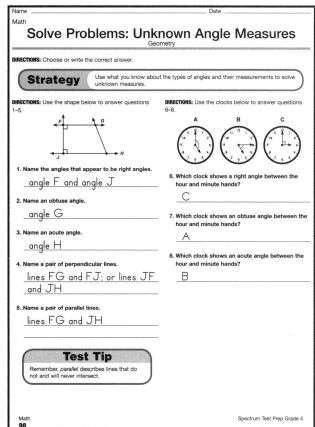

1. Name the angles that appear to be right angles.

angle F and angle J

2. Name an obtuse angle.

angle G

3. Name an acute angle.

angle H

4. Name a pair of perpendicular lines.

lines FG and FJ; or lines JF and JH

5. Name a pair of parallel lines.

lines FG and JH

DIRECTIONS: Use the clocks below to answer questions 6–8.

A   B   C

6. Which clock shows a right angle between the hour and minute hands?

C

7. Which clock shows an obtuse angle between the hour and minute hands?

A

8. Which clock shows an acute angle between the hour and minute hands?

B

Test Tip
Remember, *parallel* describes lines that do not and will never intersect.

98

Classify Two-Dimensional Figures
Geometry

DIRECTIONS: Choose or write the correct answer.

Strategy Use the properties of two-dimensional figures to solve problems.

EXAMPLE
Two-dimensional figures can be classified based on the presence or absence of parallel or perpendicular lines or the presence or absence of angles of a certain size.

EXAMPLE
This figure is a trapezoid. One pair of opposite sides is parallel. It has no perpendicular lines. It has no right angles.

This figure is a rectangle. Two pairs of opposite sides are parallel. It has perpendicular lines. It has 4 right angles.

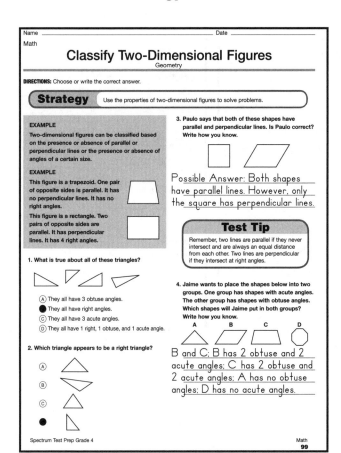

1. What is true about all of these triangles?

A They all have 3 obtuse angles.
● They all have right angles.
C They all have 3 acute angles.
D They all have 1 right, 1 obtuse, and 1 acute angle.

2. Which triangle appears to be a right triangle?

A
B
C
●

3. Paulo says that both of these shapes have parallel and perpendicular lines. Is Paulo correct? Write how you know.

Possible Answer: Both shapes have parallel lines. However, only the square has perpendicular lines.

Test Tip
Remember, two lines are parallel if they never intersect and are always an equal distance from each other. Two lines are perpendicular if they intersect at right angles.

4. Jaime wants to place the shapes below into two groups. One group has shapes with acute angles. The other group has shapes with obtuse angles. Which shapes will Jaime put in both groups? Write how you know.

A   B   C   D

B and C; B has 2 obtuse and 2 acute angles; C has 2 obtuse and 2 acute angles; A has no obtuse angles; D has no acute angles.

99

Classify Two-Dimensional Figures
Geometry

DIRECTIONS: Choose or write the correct answer.

Strategy Draw a picture and use the properties of lines and angles to describe it.

DIRECTIONS: Use the information and shapes below to answer questions 5 and 6.

5. In the space below, use any combination of these basic shapes to create a drawing of a person, place, or thing.

Answers will vary.

6. Describe the picture you drew. Use terms such as acute angle, obtuse angle, right angle, parallel lines, and perpendicular lines in your description.

Possible Answer: Any description that includes the shapes used and a description of some attributes of the shapes, e.g. "I used a triangle and two squares to make the body of a person. The triangle has no right angles, but the squares have 4 right angles each."

100

Page 101

Identify Symmetry
Geometry

DIRECTIONS: Choose or write the correct answer.

Strategy Use the properties of symmetry to answer questions.

EXAMPLE
An object or shape has a line of symmetry when the two sides can be folded along a line and match perfectly. Each side is a mirror image of the other. For example:

This rhombus has two lines of symmetry.

This arrow has one line of symmetry.

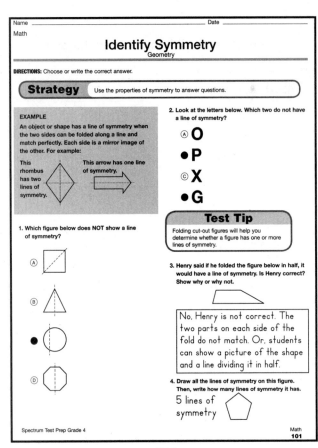

1. Which figure below does NOT show a line of symmetry?

Ⓐ Ⓑ ● Ⓓ

2. Look at the letters below. Which two do not have a line of symmetry?

Ⓐ O
● P
Ⓒ X
● G

Test Tip
Folding cut-out figures will help you determine whether a figure has one or more lines of symmetry.

3. Henry said if he folded the figure below in half, it would have a line of symmetry. Is Henry correct? Show why or why not.

No, Henry is not correct. The two parts on each side of the fold do not match. Or, students can show a picture of the shape and a line dividing it in half.

4. Draw all the lines of symmetry on this figure. Then, write how many lines of symmetry it has.

5 lines of symmetry

101

Page 102

Strategy Review
Math

In this section, you will review the strategies you learned and apply them to practice the skills.

Strategy Look for key words in word problems that help you determine which operation to use.

EXAMPLE
Eli's favorite macaroni and cheese recipes uses $\frac{5}{8}$ of a pound of cheese for the sauce and another $\frac{2}{8}$ of a pound shredded and sprinkled on top. How much cheese did Eli use altogether? If Eli started with 1 pound of cheese, how much is left? Show your work.

First, identify key words that tell you what operations to use.
The word "altogether" suggests addition.
The word "left" suggests subtraction.
Then, write and solve an equation to show how much Eli used.
$\frac{5}{8} + \frac{2}{8} = \frac{7}{8}$ pound of cheese used.
Then, write and solve an equation to show how much Eli has left.
$1 - \frac{7}{8} = \frac{8}{8} - \frac{7}{8} = \frac{1}{8}$ pound of cheese left.

1. Rory poured an equal amount of cider into 3 cups from a 2-liter jug. He had 1,100 milliliters of cider left after pouring the 3 cups. How much cider did Rory pour into each cup?

Ⓐ 266 milliliters
Ⓑ 300 milliliters
● 366 milliliters
Ⓓ 400 milliliters

Explain what operations you used, and identify the key words that helped you choose those operations.

Possible Answer: I used subtraction and division. The key words were "left" (subtraction) and "equal" (division).

2. Sophie buys 2 t-shirts. Each t-shirt costs $6.75. She pays with a $20 bill. How much change does Sophie get back?

● $6.50
Ⓑ $6.75
Ⓒ $7.50
Ⓓ $7.75

Explain what operations you used, and identify the key words that helped you choose those operations.

Possible Answer: I used multiplication and subtraction. The key words were "each" (multiplication) and "change" and "get back" (subtraction).

102

Page 103

Strategy Review
Math

Strategy Use drawings, graphs, or number lines to understand and solve a problem.

EXAMPLE
Mariah is fencing her garden to keep bunnies from eating the vegetables. She has 45 feet of fencing. The sides of the garden are 15 feet, 5 feet, 15 feet, and 5 feet. Does Mariah have enough fencing to go all of the way around her garden? Write or draw a picture to show how you know.
First, draw a picture to help you visualize the problem.

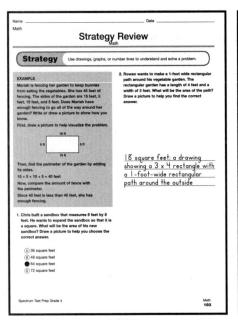

Then, find the perimeter of the garden by adding its sides.
$15 + 5 + 15 + 5 = 40$ feet
Now, compare the amount of fence with the perimeter.
Since 40 feet is less than 45 feet, she has enough fencing.

1. Chris built a sandbox that measures 6 feet by 8 feet. He wants to expand the sandbox so that it is a square. What will be the area of his new sandbox? Draw a picture to help you choose the correct answer.

Ⓐ 36 square feet
Ⓑ 48 square feet
● 64 square feet
Ⓓ 72 square feet

2. Rowan wants to make a 1-foot wide rectangular path around his rectangular garden. The rectangular garden has a length of 4 feet and a width of 3 feet. What will be the area of the path? Draw a picture to help you find the correct answer.

18 square feet; a drawing showing a 3 x 4 rectangle with a 1-foot-wide rectangular path around the outside

103

Page 104

Strategy Review
Math

Strategy Organize and display data to interpret them.

EXAMPLE
A tea shop tracks the sizes of cups of tea ordered. On Tuesday morning, customers order the following sizes:
small, small, medium, small, large, large, large, medium, medium, large, large, medium
Use a line plot to organize the data.
First, label the line plot with the range of data.
Then, add X's to show the data.

		X
X		X
X	X	X
X	X	X
small	medium	large

Now, you can use your line plot to answer questions about the data.
1. How many people ordered cups of tea?
Answer: 12
2. What size tea was ordered most often?
Answer: large
3. What size tea was ordered least often?
Answer: small

EXAMPLE
A food cart sells 29 sandwiches at lunch on Monday. Nine of the sandwiches are ham. Nineteen of the sandwiches are turkey. The rest of the sandwiches are vegetarian. The food cart also sells 25 bags of chips and 34 drinks. How many vegetarian sandwiches did the food cart sell?
What is the given information?

A food cart sells 29 sandwiches at lunch on Monday. Nine of the sandwiches are ham. Nineteen of the sandwiches are turkey. The rest of the sandwiches are vegetarian. The food cart also sells 25 bags of chips and 34 drinks.
What are you being asked to find?
the number of vegetarian sandwiches sold
Is any of the given information extra, or not needed?
Yes, we do not need to know the day, time, number of bags of chips, or number of drinks sold.

1. A music teacher orders sheet music for each student in her class. There are 34 students in the class. She places 4 pieces of music in each student's folder. The folders cost $1.95 each. How many pieces of sheet music did the teacher order? *What is the given information?*

A music teacher orders sheet music for each student in her class. There are 34 students in the class. She places 4 pieces of music in each student's folder. The folders cost $1.95 each.

What are you being asked to find?

How many total pieces of sheet music were ordered?
Is any of the given information extra, or not needed?
Answer: Yes, we do not need to know how much the folders cost.

104

Page 105

Strategy Review
Math

Strategy Use rules, properties, or formulas to solve problems.

EXAMPLE
Jackson painted a door that was 8 feet by 3 feet. Use the formula for area, $A = l \times w$, to find the area of the door Jackson painted.
First, write the formula for the area of rectangle.
$A = l \times w$
Put the measurements into the formula.
$A = l \times w = 8 \times 3 = 24$
The area of the wall is 24 square feet.

1. A path through Walt's garden is 30 feet long and 4 feet wide. What is the area of the path? Show your work.

$A = l \times w = 30 \times 4 = 120$ square feet

2. Rectangle A has a length of 5 centimeters and a width of 2 centimeters. What is the area of Rectangle A?

Ⓐ 7 cm
Ⓑ 10 cm
Ⓒ 7 square cm
● 10 square cm

Rectangle B has a length of 4 centimeters and a width of 3 centimeters. What is the area of Rectangle B?

12 square centimeters

Is Rectangle A larger or smaller than Rectangle B? Use numbers to prove your answer is correct.

Rectangle B is larger. Because Rectangle A has an area of 10 square centimeters and Rectangle B has an area of 12 square centimeters, and 12 is greater than 10, Rectangle B has a greater area and is larger.

3. The formula for perimeter is $P = 2l + 2w$. If a rectangular painting has a length of 18 inches and a width of 12 inches, what is its perimeter?

Ⓐ 30 inches
● 60 inches
Ⓒ 80 inches
Ⓓ 120 inches

Strategy
Read word problems carefully to identify the given information and what you are being asked to find.

105
